# YOUR CHILD
# AT PLAY

*Two to Three Years*

# YOUR CHILD AT PLAY

## Two to Three Years

~~~~~~~~~~~~~~~~~~~~~~~

*Growing Up, Language, and the Imagination*

SECOND EDITION

## MARILYN SEGAL, PH.D.

Foreword by WENDY MASI, PH.D.,
Director of the Family Center at Nova Southeastern University

NEWMARKET PRESS    NEW YORK

*In memory of my father, A.L. Mailman, lover of children and master of child play.*

*A Mailman Family Center Book, published by Newmarket Press, drawn from research conducted at Nova Southeastern University, Ft. Lauderdale, Florida.*

This book is published simultaneously in the United States of America and in Canada.

SECOND EDITION

10   9   8   7   6   5   4   3   2   1

Library of Congress Cataloging-in-Publication Data

Segal, Marilyn M.
    Your child at play. Two to three years / Marilyn Segal.—2nd ed.
        p.   cm.
    Includes index.
    ISBN 1-55704-336-1 (hardcover). —ISBN 1-55704-332-9 (pbk.)
    1. Child development.   2. Child rearing.   3. Play.   4. Learning
I. Title
    HQ767.9.S43  1998
    649'.122—dc21                                                97-48830
                                                                 CIP

*The author gratefully acknowledges the continuing grant from the A.L. Mailman Family Foundation, Inc., which supported the writing of this book*

QUANTITY PURCHASES
Companies, professional groups, clubs, and other organizations may qualify for special terms when ordering quantities of this title. For information, write to Special Sales, Newmarket Press, 18 East 48th Street, New York, NY 10017; call (212) 832-3575; or fax (212) 832-3629.

Photo credits:

Lisa Nalven Photography. pp. 3, 4, 5, 8, 11, 16, 18, 19, 21, 22, 23, 25, 26, 35, 37 bottom, 40, 46, 48, 50, 51, 58, 62, 64, 68, 70, 74, 75, 81, 85, 91, 93, 95, 98, 102, 103, 105, 106, 109, 112, 119, 120, 122, 125, 131, 136, 137, 141, 146, 151, 154, 157, 162, 165, 169, 172, 173, 175, 176, 179, 180, 182, 183, 186, 187, 189, 193, 194, 200, 202, 203, 208, 209, 213, 215, 219
Bill Sarchet: pp. 24, 30, 37 top, 44, 65, 67, 69, 76, 77, 101, 117, 118, 130, 134, 140, 145, 147, 150, 155, 185, 191, 196, 197
Betty Bardige: p. 27Book design by M. J. DiMassi.

# *Acknowledgments*

~~~~~~~~~~~~~~~~~~~~~~~~~~~~~~~~~~~~~~~~~~~~~~~~~~~~

This book is a collaborative effort.

WENDY MASI, PH.D., Director of the Family Center at Nova Southeastern University, is my toughest critic. She raked through the manuscript with a fine-tooth comb and weeded out passages that were inaccurate or unclear. Dr. Masi has three delightful children of her own, who just happen to be my grandchildren.

RONI LEIDERMAN, PH.D., Director of Nova Southeastern University's Family Institute, has years of intimate experience with families of very young children. She and her staff tried out all the suggested activities with parents and babies, and helped me make appropriate changes. She identified cooperative families with adorable children to participate in our photo sessions.

ANN MCELWAIN, M.B.A., Director of Marketing and Product Development at the Family Center at Nova Southeastern University, assumed the major responsibility for implementing the photo sessions. She has an uncanny way of convincing babies to do the right thing at the right time.

SUZANNE GREGORY, my most valuable assistant, has the talent to decipher my handwriting and incorporate volumes of new material and rewrites into a manageable manuscript.

# Foreword

~~~~~~~~~~~~~~~~~~~~~~~~~~~~~~~~~~~~~~~~~~~~

*Your Child at Play* is a series of books about the joy of playing with your child. When you and your child play together, you are enhancing your child's creativity and imagination, and encouraging flexible thinking. You are also getting back in touch with your own childhood, discovering a playful part of yourself that may have been buried through the years. But most important, you're connecting with your child. You are creating a bond of intimacy that will keep you and your child together in spirit, even through the often stormy teenage years.

The author of this series, Marilyn Segal, is an expert in child development, a noted professor, author, lecturer, researcher, and the founder of Nova Southeastern University's Family Center in Ft. Lauderdale, Florida, devoted to strengthening the family and enhancing the ability of parents and caregivers to nurture children. She is also a mother and grandmother whose heart and soul is invested in children, and believes more than anything in the power of play. Her home is filled with blocks, trains, books, crafts, and dolls, carefully selected so that they will be loved by all her children. Her grandchildren spend hours playing with her dollhouse and Brio set, weaving magical special worlds to which only they and their Nana are privy.

This book series is special because their author is special. She is a five foot, ninety pound powerhouse, who believes that everyone should experience the joy of play, and that playing together is at the heart of every relationship. She is my mother, my mentor, my friend. Her simple message "play together, grow together" is as powerful as it is succinct. Enjoy the books, follow your heart, and you will all have fun.

—Wendi Masi, Ph.D., Director of the Family Center
at Nova Southeastern University

# Contents

# Introduction

~~~~~~~~~~~~~~~~~~~~~~~~~~~~~~~~~~~~~~~~~~~~~~~~

*"Do you want to know about our Heather? Well, she does everything two-year-olds are supposed to do. She stamps, pouts, bites, whines, pulls the dog's tail, and colors on the wallpaper. She's stubborn, pesty, exasperating, captivating, and adorable. As a matter of fact, she's like New England weather. If you don't like what's going on . . . wait a minute."*

This thumbnail description of a two-year-old, provided by a doting father, captures some of the salient qualities of a two-year-old's behavior. Between two and three years of age, children make dramatic strides in every facet of development. Their language grows in leaps and bounds, their play becomes more imaginative, and new physical, intellectual, and social skills emerge. As two-year-olds demonstrate these capabilities, the family's expectations increase. Quite naturally, there are times when a child and a family are out of phase. When the family expects grown-up behavior, the two-year-old acts like a baby. When the family expects compliant behavior, the two-year-old wants to be boss.

Living with a two-year-old can be a challenge. It can also be lots of fun. In the course of writing this book we visited over fifty parents who had two-year-old children. As we watched parents interact with their child, we recognized differences in both mood and behavior. Some of the children seemed playful, happy, and easygoing, while others displayed more challenging behaviors like whining, noncompliance, and throwing tantrums.

In the course of our observations, we also recognized differences among parents. Some parents were easygoing, setting few rules or limits. Some parents were controlling, insisting that their two-year-old "toe the line." Other parents set limits for their child, but were playful and matter of fact. Not surprisingly, parents who were playful with their child had children who were playful and even tempered.

*Your Child At Play* could just as well be titled "Playful Parenting." It contains hundreds of anecdotes contributed by parents of two-year-olds. These anecdotes, in almost every case, exemplify playful strategies for inviting compliance and encouraging children to explore, to master new skills, and to engage in imaginative play.

The intimate involvement with the parents and children described in this book has been a rewarding experience. We believe the potential of most young children has not been fully tapped; however, our conviction that parents can tap this potential has been confirmed. Each family that we visited gave us new ideas and provided us with new insights. We would like, through this text, to share our sense of discovery with the reader.

# EXPLORATIONS

*Lisa looked up quickly as her mother entered the bedroom.*

*"Lisa, what are you doing with that good perfume? Oh, no! You naughty girl! You poured it all out."*

*Lisa's mother was too upset to explain her feelings any further. She gave Lisa a good scolding and sent her to her room. "Things like this always seem to happen when I'm on the phone," she thought. "And why didn't I have the sense to put that perfume in a safer place?"*

Exploration means playing with objects and learning about them in the process. As soon as they are able, children start

to explore the world by manipulating the objects around them. Their ability to explore grows as they become stronger, more coordinated, and more determined. By the age of two, most children are not easily deterred from their goals. Lisa wanted to play with the perfume, and she knew exactly when to go into her mother's bedroom and how to get up on the dresser. It was hard to get the little cap unscrewed, but her perseverance was rewarded.

There are moments when every parent is upset by a child's exploration. It seems that exploration always means playing with things that are off-limits. It certainly is true that two-year-old children tend to be most interested in the very objects with which they are not allowed to play. Lisa's mother was particularly angry because she felt her daughter knew better than to play with the perfume, and that her behavior was an act of defiance.

The exploration of two-year-olds can turn into defiance. Children at this age are sophisticated enough to tease or even get back at a parent by getting into things they shouldn't. In extreme cases, children are continually involved in this kind of rebellion. They see the world in terms of confrontation, and they build up their sense of accomplishment by breaking the limits set by parents.

Fortunately, most inappropriate exploration is not an expression of defiance. Lisa may merely have succumbed to temptation, as we all do at times. Perhaps she was trying to imitate her mother by putting on some perfume. Often, a forbidden object is explored not so much because it is forbidden, but because it represents a chance to imitate adults, to participate in the grown-up world.

Exploration has two faces. When we look at it one way, we see the possibility of conflict between children and parents as they clash over restrictions and rules. When we look at its other face, we see the possibility of cooperation as children learn from their parents how to master skills and make new discoveries. Use of the perfume bottle may become a recurring battle at Lisa's house, or it may become a learning opportunity. Perhaps Lisa can put on a drop of perfume while her mother supervises, or perhaps she can have her own bottle of inexpensive perfume to put on when she wishes.

Whether exploration leads to confrontation or cooperation depends on children as well as parents. Some children are especially independent, active, or curious. Some children don't understand the verbal explanations their parents give them about the rules for exploration. The situation is different in every family. There is no one way for parents to substitute cooperation for confrontation, and even if families are relatively successful in avoiding confrontation situations will always arise in which there is no way to avoid it. A certain amount of conflict over exploration is inevitable.

There is a subtle but unmistakable difference in emphasis between the exploration of the one-to-two-year-old and the exploration of the two-to-three-year-old. By the age of two years, children are less concerned with experimentation and more concerned with mastering skills. Instead of trying a whole bag of manipulative tricks on an object, the two-year-old child practices skills associated with that object. Keisha, for example, was very interested in exploring her mother's lipstick. Most of the time she did not try to squash the lipstick, break it into pieces, or smear it on the walls. Instead she practiced making the lipstick go up and down in the tube and spreading it on her lips.

In this section we look at the nature of two-year-olds' exploration from several different perspectives: investigating their world, exploring new territory, and discovering new things.

# CHAPTER 1

# *Investigations*

~~~~~~~~~~~~~~~~~~~~~~~~~~~~~~~~~~~~~

*Sabrina's mother welcomed Aunt Sarah who had come to visit from out of town. "What a beautiful collection of Hummel figurines," Aunt Sarah commented as she walked into the living room. At this moment Sabrina, age two and a half, came into the living room. Her aunt greeted her with a big hug.*

*"Oh, she is so adorable," Aunt Sarah remarked. "And how she's grown. But aren't you concerned about leaving those Hummel figurines on the table? Two-year-olds love to get their hands on things."*

*"No problem," Sabrina's mother assured her. "Sabrina has learned that things in the living room are off limits and not to touch."*

*"Well, I have a present she can touch," her aunt responded, as she pulled a teddy bear out of her bag and gave it to Sabrina. Sabrina put the teddy bear on the floor and put her hands behind her back. She had learned quite well that things in the living room were not to be touched.*

Sabrina's aunt was right about two-year-olds. They are full of curiosity and determined to investigate. At the same time, her mother was right about a two-year-old's capacity to learn rules. The problem was that Sabrina had learned the "no touching" rule too well. When children are not allowed to touch, their curiosity is squelched and opportunities to learn are reduced.

Through their investigations, children store up information that fuels new learning and serves as the basis of concept development. In this chapter, we focus on three types of investigations: visual (On the Lookout), spatial (Filling and Emptying), and part-whole relationships (Finding Out How Things Work).

# ON THE LOOKOUT

*Angelo was looking out the window. "Mommy," he shouted excitedly, "you got to see.*
*Ball's in the sky."*
*"It does look like a ball," his mother agreed, "but it is really the moon."*

When we think about the exploration of two-year-olds, we get a picture of incessant activity: running from one room to another, jumping on the bed, piling toys in the middle of the room. Exploration is all of this, but it is also more. Even when young children like Angelo are sitting quietly, they explore the world with their eyes. They are not involved in mental reflection, as adults often are, but they are very much tuned into the immediate environment.

Visual investigation occurs all the time, but it is most noticeable when children are restricted from moving around. The outstanding example is riding in the car. "I see a crane. Boy, that's a big one! Pow! Splash!" Shawn described the sound of the crane's bucket hitting the water as it dipped to scoop up another load of gravel. When Shawn rode in the car, he was happy as long as a crane could be found every ten minutes or so. Luckily there were a lot of gravel pits in the neighborhood.

Many children are like Shawn in that they look for particular objects while riding in the car. Heather looked for cement mixers; Jennifer looked for cows; Erik looked for fire hydrants. This kind of behavior is one indication of how the exploration of the toddler turns into a sense of mastery in the two-year-old. Instead of just watching the scenery go by, two-year-olds try to master the visual environment by actively searching for favorite sights. And, like Shawn, if the scenery becomes too dull, the children lose interest in visual exploration. They lose the sense of being in control.

Finding objects that are similar or matching is an important emerging skill. Children who match objects or give two ob-

jects the same name have recognized salient features that make
the objects alike. The moon is a yellow thing in the sky, whether
it is a half moon or a full moon. Two cement mixers have the
same name even if they are different colors or different shapes.
Finding similar objects is a favorite activity at the dinner table,

where two-year-olds are confined to their chairs. One night when company was coming, Jeremy's mother set the table with dark green glasses, thinking that Jeremy would be happy to get an adult glass instead of his usual plastic one. But Jeremy was not fooled so easily. "I want beer," he announced as soon as the meal began. The white liquid in his glass obviously did not match the bubbly stuff in everyone else's glass.

Matching is often stimulated by a negative presence, something undesirable that the child wants to avoid. Suzanne demonstrated her matching skill by fishing out the peas in her vegetable soup and dropping them unceremoniously on the floor. Christopher, who was distressed about a hole in his pocket, checked all his other pockets, as well as his father's pockets, to see if they had holes. Erik did not like the way the label in one of his shirts rubbed against his neck. He checked a shirt his mother was about to buy to make sure it didn't have a scratchy label.

## Watching for Changes

A number of parents reported that their children were interested in watching the sky. The sky is relatively uncluttered, and this may be why two-year-old children are attracted to it. Perhaps it is simply the majesty of the sky. In any event, there are interesting objects in the sky. Two-year-olds are like toddlers in that they watch the movements of birds and airplanes. In addition, many of them are attentive to clouds, the sun, and the moon.

Swings provide favorite vantage points for watching the sky. Most two-year-olds have not really learned to pump the swing and, as an adult pushes them, they have ample opportunity for sky gazing. Swinging higher and higher, it must seem as if they are actually going up to meet the sky. Looking down is interesting, too, especially on a sunny day. "I see my shadow," Nicole chanted to herself. "Where you go, shadow?" she playfully mused, as the shadow passed out of sight beneath her feet. As it reappeared on the back swing, Nicole watched it move. "I see you now, you silly shadow."

Shadows are mysterious phenomena that are very intriguing to children. They change their shapes on walls, grow long at night, and disappear altogether on some days. But they make good companions, always ready to play "Follow the Leader" and always right in step.

The world is full of physical changes that we take for granted but which two-year-old children see as fresh and exciting. One of the most common, and yet still fascinating, is the movement of water down a drain. The water seems to move with a will of its own, carrying along an entourage of bubbles and debris. Dropping a stone in a pool of water is similar. At first there is an interesting "pfloop" and then the rock disappears, swallowed up in a pattern of ripples.

Melting is another surprising event. Stacey likes to watch ice cubes disappear in her bowl of soup. Ice cubes in soup have been a ritual at her house ever since the first time Stacey had burned her mouth on hot soup. Since then Stacey has asked for the ice even when she hasn't wanted to eat the soup. Andrew watched a burning candle fill up with melted wax, which then dripped slowly down the side. From repeated burnings, the base of the candle looked like a multicolored waterfall. Andrew wanted to touch the wax as it assumed its new shape at the bottom of the candle, but he had learned from past experience just to watch.

Probably the most dramatic physical change two-year-olds watch is bleeding. Suddenly bright red liquid covers the skin, emerging effortlessly from a break that often is not visible. Many children eventually develop a fear of blood, but more frequently the reaction among two-year-olds is one of fascination.

As Jeannette exclaimed when she saw the blood from a cut on her leg, "What is that?" She wanted to know where it came from and listened attentively to a brief description of her insides. Thinking that her father would be just as overwhelmed by the discovery of blood, she kept telling her mother all afternoon, "I want to show Daddy when he gets home."

Not as dramatic, but still interesting, is the scab formed by dried blood. Two-year-old children are forever on the lookout for scratches and scrapes on themselves and other people. Scabs are special body parts that come and go. Each one serves as a conversation piece for a few days and then fades away.

In discussing visual exploration, we have described only a few of the interesting sights that young children notice and comment on. These examples are not meant to suggest that two-year-old children are supposed to notice such things. Every child sees something different. However, two-year-olds do have certain visual abilities in common. They can search actively for favorite objects; they are aware of interesting movements and physical transformations going on around them; and they like to match and generalize. For parents, the exciting part is to watch what their children see in the world and to share in the sense of discovery.

Often parents can suggest a new watching activity. Jason was interested in the contrast between light and shadow. One night, after watching slides, his father showed him a shadow game. He held Jason's teddy bear in front of the light from the projector, and a teddy bear shadow appeared on the screen. Jason got the idea and tried casting shadows of his other toys. Kyle's mother suggested a watching activity by giving Kyle a flashlight in a dimly lit room. The spot of light was like a living thing, and Kyle and his mother enjoyed describing its antics: "It's flying up to the ceiling! Look, the light is jumping on the piano! Oh, it's sleepy, it's lying on the floor."

# FILLING AND EMPTYING

One of the preferred pastimes of toddlers is emptying: they clear bookcases, pour milk on the floor, overturn wastebaskets. Two-year-olds continue and expand upon this theme. Taller, stronger, and more agile, they can get into heavy drawers, open closet doors, and climb up on high shelves. As Amy's mother described it, "Amy has graduated to drawers and linen closets." Because of a child's passion for emptying, particular spots in the house may be "out of order" for a while.

In general, however, the emptying behavior of two-year-olds differs in characteristic ways from that of toddlers. Emptying for its own sake diminishes. Instead, emptying is often part of a larger plan. The children are looking for specific objects, and emptying simply represents the fastest way to search. When she emptied the dressers, Amy was looking for her mother's makeup and jewelry.

In many cases, emptying serves as a prelude to filling. Most two-year-olds are engrossed in mastering the skills involved in filling, which usually is more acceptable than emptying. Filling behavior is stimulated by interesting containers. Christopher was not the only child we observed packing and unpacking an old purse. He talked to himself about his work. "Put it straight, crayons fit, this crayon fits." Purses have several advantages. They are important adult objects, they are a challenge to open and close, and they can be carried around when they are full. The world is full of other interesting containers: small suitcases, shopping bags, crayon boxes, plastic bottles, milk cartons, envelopes. New opportunities are discovered all the time.

Just as a special container stimulates filling and emptying, so does an unusual content. Two-year-old children enjoy filling a container with small items, such as pieces of macaroni, poker chips, shells, or costume jewelry. Liquid is by far the most in-

triguing material. Here, again, we see the change in emphasis from experimentation to mastery. Toddlers love to pour out cups of water, milk, juice, or other liquids. With two-year-olds, the emphasis is on pouring liquid into a cup or other container. Parents repeatedly told us about two-year-olds getting into the refrigerator in order to pour a glass of refreshment for themselves. This activity was both an exciting way to fill a container and an important way to express independence, and the children were quite upset when their parents tried to take over.

A two-year-old's ability to fill containers with water can become an obsession when the child learns to turn on faucets. Angelo was constantly at the kitchen sink trying to fill glasses with water. For several months, Erik spent his bathtime draining the tub and then refilling it. Jodi liked to sneak into the bathroom and fill the sink until it overflowed.

Filling and emptying containers of water is a theme with many variations. Brenan watered the plants outside with a hose, filling the pots with water and watching it sink out of sight. Brandon, who had learned to pour water from a sprinkling can, enjoyed sprinkling his parents when they took a bath. Kori found a unique way to fill a pan with water: squatting in the snow and catching the drops from a melting icicle.

Two-year-olds play with sand and mud much as they do with water. They fill containers and then pour out the contents. Under the tutelage of adults, children may help make sand cakes or mud pies but, in general, the focus is not on construction. Instead, children are caught up in manipulating these elusive materials and experiencing their peculiar qualities.

# FINDING OUT HOW THINGS WORK

Like filling and emptying, finding out how things work is a significant preoccupation of two-year-olds. They are interested in both the intricacies of machines and the workings of mechanical toys. From the point of view of a two-year-old, things that move by themselves are mysteries that must be solved.

## *Machines*

The preeminent machine in our culture is the automobile. From an early age, most children want to operate this machine. Between the ages of two and three, a child may learn to insert the ignition key, honk the horn, and turn on the lights, wipers, and car radio. The outstanding aspect of pretend driving, though, is turning the steering wheel. Two-year-olds want to steer all kinds of vehicles: the tractor lawn mower in a department store, the bulldozer sitting idle in the vacant lot next door, the neighbor's motorcycle. Marguerita's uncle let her climb inside his new car. She voiced the sentiment of many two-year-olds when she said, "This car is mine."

Lisa really wanted to drive the family car. When she found out there was no way her parents would let her in the front seat, she became the back seat driver. "Got to stop, coming to a light. Go slow, this road is bumpy." When her mother did not follow her instructions she kicked the front seat, which she knew would annoy her mother.

## *Computers*

As parents of two-year-olds know, a computer is an especially attractive machine. You can manipulate the keyboard, watch the images on the monitor, and listen to different noises. Although parents want their children to become computer literate at an early age, they are not likely to want their child to use the computer as a toy. One solution is to put the computer "to

sleep" except for those special minutes when you and your child can play "computer." Jermaine was allowed to push the mouse and change the image on the screen. Alesha was allowed to push the shift bar to turn a storybook page.

## Mechanical Toys

The major way we handle the desire of two-year-olds to operate machines is to give them toy substitutes. Nearly every two-year-old has a toy telephone to compensate for not being allowed to play with the real one. We give young children toy radios, cameras, tape players, and even television sets. From an adult viewpoint, these substitutions are often rather pathetic as machines, but most two-year-olds seem happy as long as a toy telephone makes a little jingle or a toy radio plays a simple tune.

When we visited Linn Su, she showed us her tape player. As soon as one tape began, she pulled it out and put in a new one. Manipulating the tape player was more fun than listening

to the music. The same thing happened with the Viewmaster®. The excitement lay in putting the discs in the machine and pressing the advance mechanism. The pictures themselves drew only a passing glance.

Two-year-old children are interested in a variety of other mechanical toys. We noticed several children who had renewed their interest in the Jack-in-the-Box toy they had received as babies. Now they could operate the toy: push the clown down inside, close the lid and turn the crank. In a similar way, we saw children winding up musical stuffed animals that had been with them since infancy. Busy boxes were once again appealing because this time the child could easily manipulate the mechanisms and study the cause and effect relationships. There were new mechanical toys as well. Wind-up vehicles could be activated. Toys that worked according to air pressure could be made to jump. Spring-loaded toys could be operated successfully. These mechanical toys stimulate the same pattern of behavior as adult machines. An intense burst of interest is likely as the child seeks to master the skill involved in making the toy work. Once this skill is developed and the child has practiced it sufficiently, the toy loses its appeal and starts to gather dust.

## Tools

Two-year-old children are interested in tools for much the same reason as they are in machines. Tools are associated with adults, and they can be used to make something happen. In fact, tools are a kind of machine, and many modern tools are electrical. But even traditional, non-electrical tools are favorites with two-year-old children. Children try to mop the floor, rake the yard, sweep the steps, and dig a hole in the garden. Once again, manipulating the tool is more important than the quality of the outcome.

Between the ages of two and three, many children are allowed to handle hammers, screwdrivers, and wrenches. Although toy tools are available, real ones are often easier to use. The children are most successful at hammering. Abdul and Jermaine helped their father hammer out pieces of copper tubing from old air conditioners. Each boy had his own hammer and could spend as long as he liked pounding on the tubing.

Some children are unusually skilled with tools. We watched Frank, who was three years old, drive a nail, try to cut

 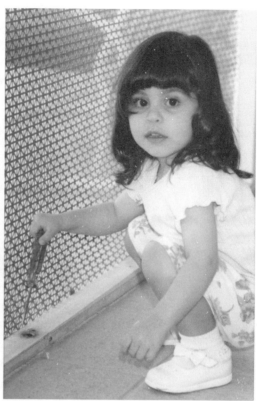

a wire with a set of pliers, and start to pry off a hubcap with a screwdriver. Frank's mother described how he always took things apart. He removed the cork seals from around the windows. His favorite toy was a truck that could be reduced to pieces. He crushed his food to bits at the table. In fact, one of the most exciting experiences of his life had been helping his grandfather take the dishwasher apart.

The outstanding function of many tools is to take things apart, and this is the characteristic that children seize on. Children like Frank, who are especially interested in mechanical relationships, will be more destructive. Shawn, for example, went beyond most children in investigating how the toilet worked. Not content to just learn how the toilet was flushed, he kept removing the back and tinkering with the mechanism inside.

When a child shows a strong inclination to take things apart, one idea is to provide an explorer box full of objects that can be dismantled. Of course, someone has to put them back together if they are to be used again.

# Exploring New Territory

Jeremy's family drove to Chicago, where his grandparents lived, three or four times a year. One Christmas, when a visit was scheduled, the family car was out of commission and they decided to go by plane. Jeremy was surprised when they arrived in Chicago an hour after they took off. "Chicago not far any more," he exclaimed.

As children move their bodies, they learn about the properties of the space around them. Identifying the relationship between speed, distance, and time, however, is beyond their comprehension. For two-year-olds, distance takes on some meaning when it is measured in terms of how far one has run or jumped. Relative position is understood more fully as children move into, out of, over, under, and through different objects.

Most interesting, however, is the two-year-old's growing awareness of the way space is organized. Beverly's mother was amazed that Beverly recognized the outside of the hairdresser's shop several months after their visit. This kind of memory for places may be surprising, but it is typical of two-year-olds. Children learn to

recognize special buildings such as the doctor's office, the local gas station, or their favorite fast food restaurant very quickly. Between the ages of two and three, they begin to remember the routes that link these familiar places. Beverly's mother discovered that Beverly would point in the direction the car should go and, more often than not, they would end up at the right place: grandmother's house, the grocery store, the beach.

A more intense kind of exploration occurs when two-year-old children investigate the spatial layout of their immediate environment. They have been familiar with the organization of their own home for a long time, and they know what to find in each room. The space right outside the house is more of an unknown quantity. Two-year-olds who are lucky enough to have a fenced-in backyard can go out and explore this territory at their leisure. They can scrutinize details such as the mud puddle under the drainpipe, the pile of bricks under the apple tree, and the garbage can near the fence. Two years of age is a good time for really getting to know the backyard and, as Shawn's mother pointed out, it can have a calming influence. Shawn was less restless inside the house after they moved to a new house with a yard.

# GOING ON A STROLL

Whether or not two-year-old children have a yard, many get a strong urge to wander beyond immediate boundaries. Alesha and her parents would often visit the neighbor next door (although her cat did not like to visit their dog). Alesha became

good friends with her neighbors, and she was allowed to go across the yard to their house on her own. It seems especially nice for two-year-olds to have this kind of relationship with neighbors. However, most parents do not want their children to go anywhere alone, even if it is just next door. Many of the parents we talked with found ways to let their children explore without exposing them to dangers. They allowed their children to ride their tricycles along the sidewalk as long as a grown-up was watching, or visit the next door neighbor if the neighbor was outside to greet them.

By far the most satisfactory compromise, from the point of view of a two-year-old, is to take a parent along on the walk. We wandered along with Angelo and his mother

on a walk around the block. During the walk, Angelo was constantly exploring. Some of the things he found interesting were
things that appeal to adults as well. He stopped to pet a neigh-

bor's dog, picked some wildflowers, and rolled a few smooth stones around in his hand. Other stops showed the special world view of a two-year-old. At one point, he circled a big tree and at another point he tried climbing a fire hydrant. The walk had no definite destination and was not confined to the sidewalk. Angelo strayed onto lawns and walked along ledges. His mother stayed nearby, reminding him of dangers, talking about the sights, and lending a helping hand when necessary. On the way back, Angelo needed more than a helping hand so his mother gave him a piggyback ride.

Exploring space is a leisurely process for two-year-old children. Angelo's walk was a success because he set the pace. Other families have described to us how unsuccessful walks can be when parents define the goals. Matthew's father was looking forward to hiking during a family vacation to the mountains. Unfortunately, the vacation was a disaster. Matthew was not interested in keeping a steady pace. He thought it was a much better idea to meander along the path, stopping to chase a butterfly or throw a twig in the stream. As a result, hiking became a hassle. The best part of the vacation, from Matthew's point of view, was wandering around every evening looking for firewood. That kind of hiking made sense.

# GOING SHOPPING

Watching Angelo on his walk, we saw a kind of playful experimentation. With each new object, Angelo seemed to be wondering, "What can I do to this? What can this do to me?" We have emphasized the two-year-old's desire to master skills through exploration, but children at this age are still expert experimenters, especially when exploring something new. They twist, pull, poke, tap, drop, throw, and even taste objects, just to see what will happen.

For many two-year-olds, a shopping excursion provides a new and exciting environment for experimentation. Stores, especially large department stores, offer interesting possibilities. No longer so overwhelmed by the hustle and bustle of shoppers or by the staggering array of merchandise, two-year-old children are more active in stores. They play with items on the shelves, hide under the clothes racks, and wander into the changing rooms. The children are interested in learning the layout of the store. During their independent jaunts, they venture further and further from parents and may set off to investigate another department.

Again, this kind of exploration can be enjoyable for both parents and children if there is plenty of time, enough time to talk to children about what they are discovering and to discuss the limitations of exploration in a store. Standing in front of a three-panel mirror or riding the escalator may be the highlight of the day. Unfortunately, shopping is often a hurried project in which the child's instinct for exploration must be subordinated to the parent's need to finish quickly.

## GOING TO CHILD CARE

Jeannette and Constance were close friends who each had a two-year-old boy. One day when they were shopping together, Jeannette told her friend that she was planning to send her son to nursery school. "Oh, are you going back to work?" Constance asked. "Not yet," Jeannette answered, "it's just that Peter loves being with other children.

Families send their two-year-olds to nursery school, day care, or play groups because they need child care, because they feel their child would enjoy the experience, or, sometimes, for both reasons. Unquestionably, two-year-olds need a predictable environment in which they feel emotionally secure and

are free to set their own direction and pace for learning. At the same time, two-year-olds can benefit from a stimulating environment with carefully planned activities, specialized materials, and a small group of new people to play with. Ideally, group settings for young children combine the qualities of both environments.

We visited several nursery schools to watch how children adjusted to different settings. A few of the child care facilities we visited were highly structured. Children were expected to sit quietly at the table waiting for instructions, stand in line to go to the bathroom, and wait until everyone was served before they started eating. Surprisingly, two-year-olds were able to cope with structure without getting out of line. At the same time, we wondered if these two-year-olds were really enjoying their day. They played with each other very little and made no demands on the teacher. They had learned to be passive and obedient, but they did not learn how to play.

In centers where the adults spent more time nurturing and less time giving instructions or managing behavior, the children were noisier and less obedient than the children in the structured center, but they seemed to be having more fun.

Although we have contrasted centers that are highly structured with centers that are more spontaneous, settings differed on several dimensions other than structure. While we recognize the difficulty of finding child care arrangements that are affordable, accessible, and open hours that meet parents' needs, we urge parents to look for the following:

- The caregivers and children look and sound happy to be there.

- Health and safety are prioritized.
- The caregiver is nurturing and spends time talking to each child.
- The environment is cheerful and organized and the children have special times for outdoor play, indoor play, nap time, snack time, and lunch.
- The caregiver has had on-the-job training in early childhood or child care.
- There is at least one adult for every five two-year-olds, and no more than ten children in a group or classroom.
- There are no more than five children of mixed ages in a home setting.
- Ten two-year-olds is an optimal group size.
- Children have a consistent caregiver.
- Parent visitation is encouraged and parents and teachers communicate on a regular basis.
- The caregivers respect and support the language, culture, and child-rearing beliefs of the family.
- A variety of age-appropriate toys and books are within reach of the children and are clean and in good repair.

Additional features that are important in choosing a successful group setting for two-year-olds include loving, enthusiastic, and energetic caregivers who have a good sense of timing and who are able to suggest a new activity or change in locale before a crisis occurs. They should call all the children by name, bend down to their level when they speak with them, and talk with children individually about "important" things such as what they are wearing, what is happening at home, or what they did yesterday. Caregivers must also have the capacity to monitor what is going on in all four corners of the room simultaneously. When there is conflict over play materials, the caregiver typically distracts the grabbing child with another toy or activity to end the conflict.

The center should have well-defined, separate physical spaces for different types of activities: places for pretend play, for motor activities, and for constructing things, as well as a fenced-in area for outdoor play. The center should be equipped with safe and intact materials and equipment including items such as wagons, rocking boats, and face-to-face swings that encourage children to play together. The play materials should be within reach of the children.

The daily schedule should provide time for free play and time for planned activity—short and non-elaborate planned activities, requiring little preparation and clean-up time. Certain activities are repeated on a daily basis to provide the children with a sense of time and sequence.

Whether the group setting is a child care home, a preschool, or a neighborhood playgroup, the principal benefit is an opportunity to develop social skills. In a good setting for two-year-olds, the major objective of play activities is to encourage peer interaction.

# CHAPTER 3

# Discovering New Things

~~~~~~~~~~~~~~~~~~~~~~~~~~~~~~~~

Alphonse's parents realized that their house was too quiet and went in search of their son. As they expected, they found him in the bathroom. "Look at the toilet," Alphonse announced. "I push this thing down, then see, the water jumps."

Having feared the worst, Alphonse's parents were relieved to see their son engaged in a scientific experiment. Though explorations can be problematic at times, parents are pleased when their child engages in experiments that lead to discoveries and new learning. In this chapter we focus on three areas of learning that interest two-year-olds: Sorting, Ordering, and Counting; New Concepts; and New Connections.

## SORTING, ORDERING, AND COUNTING

Every profession, whether it's law, construction, medicine, or landscaping, depends on the ability to sort, order, and count. The landscaper, for instance, needs to differentiate flowers from weeds, perennials from annuals, and tulip bulbs from daffodil bulbs. She also needs to know the sequence in which plants will bloom, the heights they can be expected to reach, how far apart to place the seedlings, and how many bulbs or seed packets to buy.

Even children who are under two begin to sort, order, and count. A newborn knows the difference between parent and non-parent, between smells that she likes and smells that she dislikes, between patterns that are familiar and patterns that are new. The young infant knows the sound of her father's footsteps and anticipates his arriving at her crib. She knows that when both her hands are full of toys, she has to drop one before she can pick up another.

The one-year-old is more sophisticated than the young infant in sorting, ordering, and counting. He knows that a broom is for sweeping, a hammer for banging, and a shovel for digging. He can play out a sequence of events. He can pick up a purse, fill it with odds and ends, and sling it over his shoulder. He can insist on having a cookie for each of his hands.

Between ages two and three, more sophisticated sorting, ordering, and counting skills emerge. Children learn to sort by color, to line up objects according to size, and to make connections between time and events.

Knowing that Alphonse loved both peas and carrots, his mother gave him a dish of mixed carrots and peas for dinner. She was surprised to see him just staring at the dish without even picking up the spoon. Just as she was beginning to worry about his health, Alphonse took his vegetables off the plate, placing his peas in one pile and his carrots in another. First he ate all the carrots and then all the peas. He knew the difference between peas and carrots and did not want them mixed.

When Alphonse sorted his carrots and peas, what was surprising about it was his dexterity and not the fact that he could tell them apart. Even the young two-year-old is adept at putting like objects together: socks in the sock drawer, shirts in the shirt drawer, forks in the fork place, and spoons in the spoon place. In the course of the year, the two-year-old will demonstrate more advanced sorting skills. He will learn which toys go on which shelf in the preschool and will happily participate in cleanup time. He will learn to sort things according to color and shape. The red cars go in the red garage, the blue cars go in

the blue garage; the round blocks go in the round hole, the square blocks go in the square hole.

The ordering skills that emerge in the third year are even more exciting. Coretta put three cookies in a row from big to bigger to biggest, and then, of course, took the biggest. Isabel also recognized the order of events that her teacher described: Isabel cried bitterly when her father left her in the nursery school, promising to be back pretty soon. The caregiver explained to Isabel that her Daddy would pick her up after lunch. First they would play in the classroom, next they would have cleanup time, next they would play outside in the yard, next they would have lunch, and then her Daddy would come back. Although Isabel was somewhat unsettled all morning, she did not cry or ask for her Daddy. As soon as they sat down to lunch she watched out the window to see if her Daddy was coming. The teacher's technique of talking about the order of events rather than the timing of events helped Isabel understand that her father would return and she did not have to worry.

## *Number and Shape*

Ultimately the organization of space and time depends on number concepts. Space and time are quantified in phrases such as "three miles away" and "ten minutes ago." Although two-year-olds may pick up a random phrase here and there, the application of numbers to space and time is beyond them. However, awareness of number concepts is beginning in other ways.

Numbers are mentioned most frequently in connection with age. Children learn to hold up two fingers when asked how old they are, or three if they want to indulge in a bit of wishful thinking. It will be a long time, however, before the children understand that they are talking about two years.

Although children do not grasp the meaning of two years, they may understand the idea of two fingers. Finger plays and other informal games help establish the "twoness" of the human body—two eyes, two ears, two hands, two feet. Pairing objects is almost an instinct with people, and two-year-olds are no exception. Carrying one object in the right hand and another in the left hand is a natural way to make two. Jason surprised his parents one day by placing two hair brushes on the floor and announcing "two." Soon afterwards he found two shoes to carry, two toothbrushes, and two trucks.

Children's early ability to recognize two is related to visual recognition rather than counting. If you draw a face with two noses or a dog with five legs, two-year-olds recognize that something is amiss.

In addition to recognizing certain quantities, many two-year-olds begin to count. Gillian was attracted to the animated

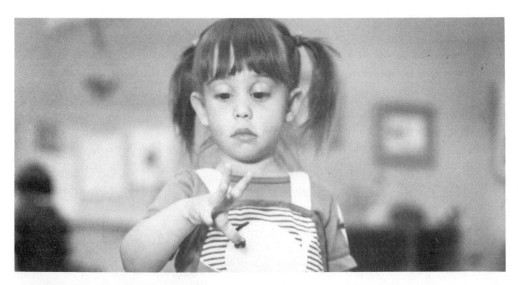

counting sequences on "Sesame Street." The machine gun rhythm, which Gillian's parents found nerve-racking, invariably caught her attention. When her father introduced the idea of counting the buttons on a new dress, Gillian responded enthusiastically.

Traditionally, the fun of counting was emphasized by rhymes such as "one, two, buckle my shoe." "Sesame Street" has shown us an even more powerful technique: shout and count. Parents have become more concerned with teaching children to count and, because of the razzle-dazzle on television, counting has become an enjoyable social activity. In addition, there are a number of excellent books that are designed to introduce counting to young children.

Early counting tends to be rote: that is, it is a language exercise in which children merely repeat number words in the proper sequence. Rote counting is not necessarily accurate. A child may skip some objects while counting others more than once. Even the rote sequence may be confused. Jason started with five instead of one. Gillian always left out seven.

With practice and assistance, some two-year-old children can learn to count accurately. Daren's mother helped him touch each picture in a counting book as they counted out loud together. Beverly's mother taught her to pick up each object and move it when counting, so that no object would be missed or counted twice.

The transition from rote to rational counting is not an instantaneous process. For many young children, the two coexist, with rational counting used when a small quantity is involved and rote counting taking over when a quantity becomes too large. Angeline, for example, had learned to count the four people in her family, and she could count four objects in other situations, as well. However, when she tried to count the presents under the Christmas tree, her deliberate counting style disappeared. She touched the packages and cheerfully recited various number sequences, as if playing a private counting game.

The range of a two-year-old's counting skills is not very important. The difference between being able to count to three versus ten is not going to matter in the years ahead. The significance of this new concept is that children are becoming aware of quantity. They are beginning to realize that there is a systematic method for counting objects, whether they come in a big bunch, a small bunch, or one at a time.

One conscientious mother we visited had been playing with her son in a pretend situation before we arrived. He was pretending that a set of plastic rings were various fish. "Find me the biggest fish," the mother requested. "No, that's not the biggest fish," the mother continued. "The biggest one is right behind you. How many fish am I holding in my hand now?" Although his mother was using an imaginative play situation to teach her son counting and ordering, she was intent on teaching her son rather than playing with him. Fortunately, later in the day this same mother resumed the fish game. This time she did not play teacher, and both mother and son had more fun.

Mother: *"Thank you for finding me the little fish. I will hide him under the rock so the big fish will not scare him."*
Child: *"Big fish scaring him. Big fish swimming, swimming, swimming."*
Mother: *"Be careful, big fish. You may get stuck under the rock."*
Child: *"Big fish swimming under the rock. Be careful swimming under the rock."*

## NEW CONCEPTS

The discoveries of a two-year-old are not limited to the properties of objects. They are beginning to recognize the relationship between their different experiences and are beginning to generalize or develop concepts about their experiences.

Isabel's mother took advantage of some quiet time to sort out the mail and get some bills paid. Isabel was playing happily in the room surrounded by a basket full of pretend food, a set of dishes, and a large collection of stuffed animals. Suddenly, Isabel's mother realized that it was too quiet in the bedroom. Did she remember to close the bathroom door? She rushed out to investigate, and, sure enough, there was Isabel sitting on the bathroom floor. Somehow or other she had found a new tube of toothpaste that her mother had put in a lower cabinet. "Look, Mommy," she said proudly as she scooped up a handful of toothpaste that she had squeezed out of the tube, "I make good ice cream."

Two-year-olds like Isabel are fascinated by transformations. The toothpaste can be squeezed out of a tube and picked

up like a dish of ice cream. Kori, who was also interested in the ways things change, stood on the sidewalk by the road completely enthralled by what she saw. The snow bank was melting and the water was running into the sewer. "I see snow water," Kori announced. Then she picked up a handful of snow and rubbed her hands together. To her delight, the snow turned into water.

Through explorations and experiments, two-year-olds are constantly making discoveries. They learn the nature of various materials and objects and learn ways that things can be restructured into new forms. The toothpaste piles up like a dish of ice cream; a handful of snow turns into water. Some things can be combined, and other things cannot. Some things break into pieces when you drop them, other things bounce, and still other things don't change at all.

The kitchen is a favorite place for learning about the properties of objects and watching combinations. Celestine was thrilled when she got a tray of eggs out of the refrigerator. One by one she picked up each egg, dropped it, and watched the yellow and white stuff make a puddle on the floor. Recognizing that Celestine wanted to help with the cooking, Celestine's mother gave her a bowl of water and an almost empty salt shaker. Celestine poured the salt into the water, mixed it with a spoon, and watched it disappear. A few minutes later she noticed some shelled peas that her mother had put on the counter. She picked up a handful of peas and threw them in the water. "Peas won't go away," Celestine announced, as she continued her vigorous stirring.

## Space and Time

A fundamental insight during the period of infancy is that objects have permanence. Rattles, bottles, and people continue to exist even if they can't be seen or touched. At two years old, children develop a new appreciation of the world's permanence. Space and time extend beyond the boundaries of immediate experience.

An awareness of far-away places is seen in different ways. Two-year-olds may be curious about people who get on planes and disappear into the sky, or they may note that the sun seems to sink into some distant hole at night. Perhaps they dimly realize that certain relatives live in a different part of the world, or that some unusual animal, such as a shark, lives far out in the ocean. Frank and Constance yelled "Grandma" every time they saw "Wild Kingdom" on television. Grandma was not part of "Wild Kingdom" but she did live in Omaha, and the twins knew that the program was sponsored by a far-away company called Mutual of Omaha.

Just as two-year-olds expand their vision of space, so do they extend their sense of time. "I rode a horse last night," Melissa told us. "She means the merry-go-round at the carnival," her mother explained, "and it wasn't really last night; it was a couple of weeks ago." Although her sense of time was not very precise, Melissa had made a critical distinction. She was able to indicate that the horse ride had not been a part of the current day's events.

The time words that two-year-olds use reflect their limited conceptual framework. Melissa was not necessarily confused when she described an experience several weeks in the past as "last night." She used "last night" to refer to any past event. Lacking a system for combining days into weeks, she found an alternative. Things happen either today, a day some time in the past, or a day some time in the future, for which Melissa used "in a couple days." Other children use "yesterday" and "tomorrow" as their all-purpose terms.

The appearance of these terms makes it possible for two-year-olds to talk about time. In turn, parents find it much easier to talk to the children about the past and the future.

However, these terms represent new concepts that are just emerging, and it is not essential that two-year-olds use them. Even without special words for the past and future, children are able to describe things that have happened and things that are going to happen.

## *Ideas About Life*

Between two and three, children begin to appreciate the special qualities of living things. Enhanced by the impressive noises they make, trucks, buses, and other machines may seem to be alive. Above all, two-year-olds are attracted to animals as another form of life, attracted and yet apprehensive, too. Animals are both exciting and frightening.

The animals two-year-olds know best are pets. A pet is accepted as a member of the family, and two-year-olds develop a special relationship with this "brother" or "sister." For one thing, the pet has the fewest privileges in the family. All sorts of restrictions are placed on its behavior, and the two-year-old is the first one to enforce these special rules. "Mittens, you bad boy," scolded Jodi. "You get off the table." Christopher took even greater delight when Pooh jumped on a visitor's lap. "Dad," he reported excitedly, "Pooh is bugging our guest."

Without question, the two-year-old's style is to boss or control the family pet. The primary means of controlling a pet is to handle it: to pet and poke it, to hug and kiss it, to carry it around. Yet behind this bossiness is a desire to make friends, to form a personal relationship with the pet. Linn Su insisted on taking her dog into the bathroom with her. Jason cried when the cat would not sit next to him and watch television.

Because young children try so hard to make friends with family pets, parents often find themselves explaining the need to be gentle. Being too rough with a pet may hurt it. On the

other hand, the animal can hurt the child by biting or scratching. These are difficult concepts for a child to understand, and they cannot be learned without trial and error. Recognizing that two-year-olds are experimenting with ways to handle animals, most families with young children seek out pets that are even-tempered and robust.

Two-year-olds are likely to extend their animal friendships to animals that are not family members. Birds are among the most common animals in any environment, and it is not unusual for a two-year-old to chase a duck or a pigeon. Although children enjoy the chase, the real object is to catch, or at least touch, the bird and make friends. Feeding an animal is another way to make contact. Children's petting zoos are ideal for this purpose.

Despite the fact that two-year-olds enjoy touching and feeding a variety of animals, there still is a strong element of fear associated with them. Kori, who was familiar with the family dog, was reluctant to pet her cousin Jennifer's cat. "Why don't you help Jennifer pet Isaac?" Jennifer's mother suggested to Kori. "I really don't think I should," Kori rationalized. "I have a cold."

One way to relate to animals without taking any chances is through an imaginative experience. Even two-year-olds who have little opportunity to meet real animals, or who are afraid of real animals, enjoy listening to an animal story. Usually the animals in a story are personified. They talk, wear clothes, and eat human food. The stories may not provide much factual information about animals, but they reinforce a young child's desire to identify with other forms of life.

From time to time, two-year-olds comment on differences between people and animals. Most often they will point out, in a disappointed tone of voice, that animals cannot really talk. Some children notice that animals do not use toilets and that many of them do not have hands. These distinctions only serve to highlight the strong affinity that young children have for animals.

It seems to us that parents play an essential role in helping two-year-olds relate to animals. Children are drawn to the variety of animal life around them, and their interest provides an opportunity for parents to encourage a respect for life. Of all the families we visited, Abdul's and Jermaine's parents most clearly expressed this feeling. During our visit, Abdul found a bug outside and, with a loud cry, he smashed it. His mother reminded him that he was not supposed to kill a bug until after he had asked his parents if it was a good bug or a bad bug. Jermaine, Abdul's three-year-old brother, knew that spiders were good bugs. Recently he had found several dead spiders in the house and commented, "Daddy's spiders are dead." On another occasion, Abdul and Jermaine had collected some snails in a can. Their father noticed one of the snails crawling out of the can and said to the boys, "Look, the snail is trying to go home." He persuaded Abdul and Jermaine to put the can on the porch so all the snails could go home, and by the next morning they were gone.

Just as two-year-olds are beginning to recognize a wider range of life, they also are becoming more aware of the life process itself. They are most aware that animals, including people, move and eat. In addition, they sometimes are exposed to the idea that life is a process of renewal, of birth and death. Questions about birth and death are inspired by direct experience. Jodi, for example, was very curious about the new baby born in her family and was verbal enough to put her puzzle-

ment into words: "Mommy, did I drink from your nipples when I was a baby? What did I do when I was inside you?"

Questions about death are less common because families try to shield children from this fact of life. When a death does occur in the immediate family, however, some two-year-olds pursue the subject. After the death of his grandmother, Jeffrey asked over and over again when they were going to get Grandma back. His mother explained what had happened, but the questions continued. Finally, she gave him a picture of his grandmother to keep by his bed, and he seemed to be satisfied. Daren, another two-year-old, found his own method of coming to terms with a grandparent's death. He had asked no questions during the funeral, and his family took it for granted that he really wasn't aware of what was going on. Then his mother noticed that he was drawing intently on a small slate. "I making Grandpa," he said to himself as he made some circular squiggles. After several minutes, he picked up the eraser, rubbed the slate vigorously, and continued with his monologue, "Where Grandpa go? Grandpa all gone!"

As two-year-olds gain new insights into themselves and other people, and as they experience the whole range of human emotions, they form a sense of themselves as individual people. They also develop a set of expectations about the world and the people in it. To a large degree, their futures will be shaped by their expectations: expecting joy, they will find it; expecting beauty, they will recognize it; and expecting love, they will experience it.

Because the two-to-three-year-old child is learning so many new things, parents are faced with an awesome responsibility and a magnificent opportunity. We can help our children feel confident about themselves and their ability to cope with new situations. We can help them discover a wider world by providing a secure home base. Perhaps most important of all, we can provide our children with a reservoir of happy memories. Sometimes the very best thing to do is to turn our backs on the future and focus on the here and now, for with every moment of joy and with every exposure to beauty we are building up good memories.

# NEW CONNECTIONS

When Melinda's mother came into the room she found Melinda sitting at her desk tearing up her checks. "What exactly are you doing?" her mother asked. "Go away. I'm working. I make money just like Daddy. You want lots of money?" Melinda asked, as she gave her mother a handful of torn checks.

Melinda's mother, who had been about to lecture her daughter, realized that Melinda was making some interesting connections. Money is something you make. Checks have something to do with money, and money is something that grown-ups like to have.

The development of language skills is the impetus for concept development. When two-year-olds understand, or at least partially understand, the language and can put words together to express their thoughts, they are well on their way to learning and describing real world connections.

Some time during the third year, children begin to grapple with the connection between going to work, making money, and having a job. Children realize that one or both parents go to a certain place and work. The nature of the work may be a mystery, but children are often aware that money is associated with work. They also begin to see that different people perform different kinds of work. Of special interest are the workers with uniforms or special hats: police officers, bus drivers, garbage collectors, barbers, construction workers.

A second set of connections involves buying and selling. Most prominent is the fact that food is bought at a grocery store. Children also learn at an early age that gas is bought at a service station. Gradually this idea expands, as the children begin to distinguish the separate functions of drug stores, hardware stores, toy stores, and so on. Some department stores carry almost everything, while other stores have only one kind of thing.

A third connection that children ponder over is the connection between things and ownership. This is a hard lesson to learn. The things in stores belong to the store until they are bought. The cars in the street belong to different people and cannot be entered at will. Even the grass along the sidewalk is the property of someone else and must be trodden on carefully.

These connections, and others like them, are not generated by any one kind of experience. They are the cumulative result of exploration of all kinds. As children try to connect these different experiences, they develop their first primitive ideas about how society works.

The importance of parents in guiding and fostering exploration has been implicit throughout this chapter. Although two-

year-old children try to conduct some of their exploration in secret, they typically want parents to pay attention to their activity and to talk with them about it. It is even better if the parents participate. As Christopher's father told us, "Christopher is happy to play with his toys as long as I play along, but if I don't pay attention to him, he will tear the place up."

Involvement with children through exploration gives parents a chance to warn their children of dangers and to explain restrictions. It also gives parents the opportunity to introduce new ideas. Exploration is not always a discovery experience. Parents can suggest a strategy for completing a puzzle, demonstrate a new way of building, or invent an action game. As long as they are not made to feel inferior, two-year-old children are eager for new ideas. The ultimate goal remains mastery, and children look to their parents to help them reach this goal.

# EVERYDAY LIVING

The routines of everyday living—sleep time, mealtime, dressing, washing up, and using the toilet—account for a large portion of the two-year-old's day. It is not surprising that when parents describe how impossible or how delightful their child is, they talk about routines.

Alphonse's dad took care of him one evening. When his mother arrived home she found father and son lying together on the bed reading a good night story. Minutes later, Alphonse was asleep and Dad described his evening with Alphonse.

"Alphonse was impossible at dinner. He refused to stay in the chair, threw peas on the floor, and picked up his juice and poured it in his hair. I expected the whole evening would be a hassle, but right after dinner everything changed. He had a wonderful time in the bathtub, put his pajamas on mostly by himself, climbed into bed, and asked me to read him a story."

In this section we look at some of the challenges and opportunities associated with the routines of everyday living: Everyday Challenges, Helping Out, and Keeping the Peace. Although we do not endorse a particular technique, we do discuss coping techniques that parents describe as successful.

# CHAPTER 4

# *Everyday Routines*

~~~~~~~~~~~~~~~~~~~~~~~~~

Jeremy's mother had just left the kitchen when she heard a very loud "uh-oh," and came rushing back. "What's the matter?" she asked, as she hurried back to the kitchen. "Mommy, milk pilled." Relieved, his mother assured him that it was just a little bit of milk and she could wipe it up in a second. "I do," Jeremy insisted. "Need a punge." As you would expect, wiping up the milk was so much fun that Jeremy spilled it again, this time, of course, on purpose.

Two-year-olds are full of surprises. They are learning new skills every day: eating by themselves, or washing their face and their toes in the bathtub, and once in a while using the potty. They are insistent about doing things by themselves, even though their idea of helping may differ from their parents'. Their intense desire, single-mindedness, insistence on having their own way, and need for power and control sometimes make them fun to live with and sometimes present a challenge. This chapter includes three sections: Sleep Time and Mealtime, Dressing and Washing Up, and Toilet Learning.

Marguerita was excited about her new big bed. Although her parents had expected that she would give them a hard time, Marguerita ate her dinner, took her bath, picked up her favorite panda, and put herself and her panda in the big bed. "Marguerita," her Dad called out. "Didn't you forget something? Didn't you forget to give your Daddy a big good night kiss?"

Parents feel ambivalent about their babies growing up. They want their two-year-olds to become more self-sufficient in managing their daily routines. At the same time, they miss the cuddling and the warm feelings that go along with taking care of a baby. Children are just as ambivalent as their parents. They want to be grown-up and in control, but at the same time they would like to be cared for like a baby.

# SLEEP TIME AND MEALTIME

## *Sleep Time*

Bedtime problems topped the list of parental concerns among the families we visited. For many families, the problem was getting the child into bed in the first place. The children's resistance seemed to stem from several factors. First, they have become aware that bedtime, like other routines, is a decision made by parents. If parents could decide it was time for bed, two-year-olds felt they could decide it was not time. In support of their view, two-year-olds could point to the fact that other members of the family did not go to bed at the same time as they did. A second reason was that the two-year-olds found it increasingly difficult to go to bed and relax at the end of the day. No longer was it easy for them to forget their memories of the immediate past or their plans for the immediate future. They wanted to hold onto the pleasures of the day and to keep playing just a little longer. Finally the two-year-olds had a new appreciation of their aloneness during sleep. Imaginary fears assailed them in the solitude of their bedroom. Why should they have to sleep by themselves while their parents get to share a bed?

Most children establish bedtime routines at an earlier age. They learn to get ready for bed by taking a bath or reading a story. They develop favorite sleeping positions and a variety of comforting behaviors, such as sucking a thumb or stroking a blanket. But these routines prove inadequate as they grow older, and going to bed becomes a recurring battle.

Some parents we interviewed tried letting the children cry themselves to sleep. While this technique was endorsed by some parents, most parents discovered that it didn't work very well. At this age children can keep in mind why they are upset and what they want to do about it. They can use words as well as screams to communicate their dissatisfaction, and frequently they climb out of their crib or bed. This is not to say that the technique never works. When they used the technique occasionally, and as a last resort, parents were able to force two-year-olds to go to sleep by ignoring them. However, very few of the parents reported that this approach resolved bedtime problems on a regular basis.

Other families went to the opposite extreme and avoided bedtime problems by eliminating any differences between two-year-olds and other family members. When it was time for the two-year-old to go to bed, all the lights in the house were turned out and everyone went to sleep, usually in the same room. Or, alternatively, two-year-olds stayed up as long as they wished. If they felt tired, they might lie down and go to sleep in the living room, right in the middle of the family circle. If they did not feel tired, they went to sleep later, when their parents went to bed.

Most of the parents we interviewed took a more moderate approach. They tried to avoid bedtime problems, but without giving up the distinction between grown-ups and young children. At the same time, they did not use their adult authority to coerce the children into compliance. The parents' general strategy was to make bedtime more attractive for a two-year-old. Some families bought a bed to replace the crib; others purchased new sheets with designs that appealed to their children. Some families took advantage of their two-year-olds' burgeoning imaginations and bought new stuffed animals and doll friends for bedtime. However, the essence of this middle-of-the-road approach was to elaborate on the bedtime ritual that had been started earlier. Parents who had read one good night story to their children found themselves reading three or four stories. Those who had settled their children with a song found their songs kept getting longer and longer.

Sometimes these elaborate bedtime routines became quite unique. For example, in Andy's family the routine was a symbolic game of Hide and Seek. First, Andy hid in his parent's bedroom and they found him; then the parents hid in Andy's bedroom and he found them. Zachary's parents held him up to the bedroom window so that he could say good night to all

the children in the neighborhood. Then he was put in his crib, whereupon he threw out all the stuffed animals except the monkey. Jodi's mother would hug Jodi, pull away, then come back for another hug and kiss. After three or four of these return hugs, she would leave the room.

For most families, bedtime routines are not preplanned by the parents but grow spontaneously as different ideas are tried out. Eventually a routine is established that satisfies both parents and children. The parents in the family feel that their particular routine is a reasonable investment of time and does not overly indulge a two-year-old child. For the two-year-olds, the elaborated routine gives them greater control over the process of going to bed, provides a pleasurable last event for the day, and minimizes their separation fears. Of course, bedtime is still subject to some hassles because the goals of parents and children often diverge. Both enjoy the intimate interaction, but parents want to move toward briefer bedtime routines, while children want to draw out this period of special attention.

The pressures that lead to elaborate bedtime routines are less evident in families when a two-year-old has older siblings. If the two-year-old slept in the same room as an older sibling, separation fears were greatly lessened. The two-year-old did not feel singled out when it was time for bed, and was not as likely to conclude that bedtime was a cruel and unusual punishment. In fact, siblings who slept in the same room often looked forward to a private period of playing and talking before they went to sleep. The parent-child routines that evolved in other families were replaced by child-child routines.

Several of the parents we visited were concerned about their children waking up in the middle of the night. Quite a few of these children seemed to be experiencing vivid dreams. They talked, yelled, and even cried as they slept, and if a dream awakened them in the middle of the night, they often had trouble going back to sleep. Children who awakened for other reasons were often frightened by the darkness and strangeness of the night and by their sense of being alone. A few of the two-year-olds took action to solve this kind of problem by themselves. They got up, wandered through the house, and went back to sleep in a more secure spot, usually in their parents' bedroom. There were parents who encouraged this response by providing alternative sleeping places in their bedroom for the children. Other parents roused themselves and took the children back to their own beds.

Once back in the two-year-old's bedroom, parents needed to find ways to help the children relax. They called attention to reassuring fixtures in the room: the night light, the familiar blanket, the favorite stuffed animal. They developed a mini-routine such as rubbing their baby's back, giving him a massage, or giving the two-year-old a drink of water or juice. Some parents reported that magical rituals calmed their children. Marguerita's father, for example, always put a magic kiss on Marguerita's forehead to chase away bad dreams. Allison's mother got rid of nighttime monsters by opening the window and pretending to throw them out. But by far the most common and most effective thing parents did was to stay in the child's bedroom until the two-year-old fell asleep or was clearly relaxed. Nothing equals the reassuring presence of parents. Some parents patted their children, some rocked their children, some lay down on the floor and took a nap.

Like bedtime routines, these various tactics for responding to middle-of-the-night waking were habit forming. Whatever parents started, children expected in the future. A brief routine, such as giving the child a drink or a magical kiss, was easy to maintain because it did not alter basic sleeping arrangements. Letting a two-year-old crawl into the parents' bed, or lying down on the child's bed until the child fell asleep, did change basic sleeping arrangements and was harder to keep up night after night. In considering how to respond to middle-of-the-night wakefulness, parents face a dilemma. The most effective techniques are also the most likely to disrupt their own sleeping patterns.

Finally, whether the problem is bedtime resistance or awakening during the night, parents need to think about their child's day. Did something happen at home that worried the two-year-old? Did he have a new experience that he found frightening? Was he concerned about being separated from his parents? Although it is not possible to avoid or take away all stressors, extra hugs and reassuring words are comforting to a two-year-old.

## *Mealtime*

Some of the happiest moments within each family are associated with eating. These include shared cooking time, birthday parties, picnics, or dinner at a fast food restaurant. On the other hand, some of the most stressful moments in a family are also associated with eating. Although no two families are alike, we found a consistent pattern in the eating problems that were reported. Parents told us repeatedly that breakfast and lunch usually went fine, but the trouble occurred at dinner.

At breakfast and lunch, different members of the family eat different cereals or sandwiches, and two-year-olds are often allowed to choose what they want to eat. At dinner time, the children are expected to eat the meal that has been prepared for the whole family. Two-year-olds know, however, that there is other food in the kitchen, and gradually they become bold enough to demand it. Heather realized that there was a can of spaghetti and meatballs in the cupboard, and in her mind it must have seemed unfair that this food could only be opened at lunch.

Dinner is different in other ways, too. For most families it is the most formal meal of the day. The meal lasts longer and children are expected to stay at the table. Brandon's father had just come back from a two-day trip. His mother had planned a particularly nice dinner and had even made it a festive occasion by placing candles on the table. Brandon sat politely at the table for the first half of the meal, but when his sister asked for more beans and his father said something to his mother that he couldn't understand, Brandon grew restless and slipped down from his youth chair. "Brandon, please stay at the table," his mother requested. "We want tonight to be a very happy time for all of us." Brandon, who saw no connection between happiness and sitting at the table, shouted "no" defiantly and dashed around the room. "Brandon," his mother cajoled, "I have a

lovely dessert for you. As soon as you finish eating your meat, you can have dessert." "I don't want my meat, I want dessert," Brandon shouted back. "Brandon," his father insisted in a firm voice, "you heard what your mother said. Now let me put you back in your chair."

Staying in his chair is not much of an issue for Brandon at breakfast and lunch. He usually watches "Sesame Street" while eating breakfast, and he likes to eat lunch on the run. Although he is not supposed to take food into the living room, he can eat a sandwich while playing in the family room or outside on the patio. Breakfast and lunch end when he is through eating. Brandon is not required to sit and wait for his sister or parents to finish. The atmosphere is casual and spontaneous. Sometimes the family eats together and other times everyone eats independently.

The formality of dinner also means that more emphasis is placed on good manners. Many two-year-olds enjoy playing with their food. Chocolate pudding, they discover, makes fine fingerpaint; bread is good for making balls; and carrots and lima beans are fun to squash. A limited amount of this play may be tolerated at breakfast or lunch, but at dinner parents expect children to use a fork instead of their fingers, to take moderate bites instead of stuffing their mouths with food, and to ask for food instead of grabbing it.

The techniques that parents use to handle mealtime problems depend both on what meal it is and on their style of parenting. Some parents believe in teaching their children to follow the rules, others are willing to bend the rules when they don't think it's worth a hassle. Still others believe that rules are unnecessary when it comes to eating.

## Rules About Eating

Parents who believe that rules about meals and snacks are important, primarily for health reasons, but also for learning good manners, set down some firm rules about eating.

- Children are not to have snacks before meals.
- Children must not eat with their fingers.
- Children must not have dessert until they have eaten their main course.
- At dinner, children must not get up until the meal is over.

While setting down reasonable rules may be effective in most situations, it also has some drawbacks. Parents may find that a rule they established may not have the effect they anticipated. In Angelo's house there was a firm rule about junk food. No sweets and only nutritious snacks were served in the house. Angelo was also expected to follow the same diet when he went out. This strategy backfired at a birthday party. Angelo was the first one to find a jar of candy and ask for a second piece of

cake. His parents recognized that the rules they established for mealtime were only respected when they were there to enforce them.

Parents who took the opposite approach and established no rules about eating also ran into problems. Coretta's parents

believed that food was not something to quarrel about and children should eat what, when, and however they wanted. Coretta's mother found herself working overtime to make breakfast for each of her children. Quite often, after she made the dish that was requested, the dish remained uneaten. "I'm not hungry," Coretta insisted after her mother had served her the eggs and sausage she had asked for. Another problem came up when Coretta was taken out to dinner at her aunt's house. "I hate beans, they're yucky. I hate that kind of hamburger. I want ice cream." When her mother told her aunt that it would be all right to give her ice cream, Coretta put her face in the bowl and lapped up the ice cream like a cat. Her parents were embarrassed and couldn't wait to get home.

Brenan's parents took a middle course. They set rules about not making a mess with food and about staying at the table in a restaurant. One day when they took Brenan out to dinner, he forgot all the rules. He poured salt and pepper on the table, ate mashed potatoes with his fingers, and slipped out of his chair and ran around the restaurant. His mother got him back in the booth by promising him a story. Remembering how much he loved "Sesame Street," she decided to tell him about Ernie.

"Ernie went out to dinner with his friends. As soon as he got to the restaurant he took a bottle of ketchup and splashed it on the wall. Next he jumped out of his chair, and took a french-fried potato off someone else's table. When Ernie came back to the table he discovered his own mashed potatoes and put a handful in his hair. Do you know what his friends said? They said, 'Ernie, we're not going to eat with you anymore until you learn to be a good Muppet.'"

Brenan calmed down as he listened to the story, and soon chimed in with his own ideas. Ernie stories became a restaurant ritual, and Brenan learned to enjoy eating properly. Although all parents can't think up Ernie stories, the technique of establishing rules, and thinking up non-punitive ways to enforce them works well most of the time.

# DRESSING AND WASHING UP

## *Dressing*

Timothy's mother greeted us at the door. "Just in time," she assured us. "I just got Timothy dressed up and ready for his picture." At that moment, Timothy strolled into the room. On top he was wearing an attractive plaid shirt neatly buttoned up; on the bottom he was wearing nothing. "Oh, no, not again," his mother said in dismay. "Ever since this kid learned to undress himself, I can't get him to keep his clothes on."

Other parents we visited had similar complaints. Their two-year-olds had mastered the ability to take their clothes off, and much of the time they preferred to go naked around the house. When it came time to get dressed, they resisted either by running away or by peeling off their clothes almost as quickly as parents could get them on. This tendency of two-year-olds to prefer nudity can lead to a power struggle over dressing. Children feel that it is their right to remain in a state of undress, while parents feel just as strongly that it is their responsibility to keep their children dressed.

Although many two-year-olds revel in nakedness, they are also intrigued by certain clothes. These clothes become important possessions and are a part of their sense of identity. Shoes are the most common example. Some children get attached to one pair of shoes and refuse to wear any others. They act as if changing to different shoes would change them in some sort of disastrous way. Kori, for example, became attached to a pair of red sneakers and insisted on wearing them with a long pink party dress at Thanksgiving dinner. Other children are more like Kyle, who decided that his sandals were for playing at the park, his sneakers were for nursery school, and his brown shoes were for McDonald's. Some children refuse to wear any shoes at all, but still insist on carrying favorites around with them.

It is understandable that shoes are promoted to positions of honor and distinction. For one thing, they go on feet, and from the moment babies first discover their own toes, feet hold

a special fascination. Furthermore, from a child's point of view, the rituals in the shoe store make the buying of shoes an awesome occasion. The child sits down in a special chair and a strange adult comes over with a big silver shining thing. The silver thing closes itself gently around the child's foot. Then the strange adult brings out an armful of boxes. This stranger keeps taking shoes out of the boxes and fitting them on until just the right shoes are found. Then, with even greater solemnity, the shoes get wrapped up and paid for. The new shoes, with their new smell and new feel, are taken home. The next day, as the shoes run and jump, they will testify to all concerned that the child has indeed grown bigger.

Recognizing that certain clothes have extra meaning for two-year-olds, most of the parents we visited did let their children help decide what to wear. Inevitably, there were some problems. From a parent's viewpoint, the children seemed excessively rigid. "Why must it be the same dress every Sunday?" thought Jeannette's mother. Jeannette was attached to a dress that had bells sewn into the hem. She called it her ring-ding dress. From a child's viewpoint, however, it may seem that parents are rather rigid in their ideas, too. Parents seem to have the peculiar notion that certain clothes do not go with each

other, like red sneakers with a pink party dress.

Even when parents do not insist that their children look stylish, limits have to be set on the free choice of clothing. There are times when children insist upon wearing something that either is or ought to be in the washing machine. There are also hot days when children decide to wear a turtleneck sweater and cold days when they would like to wear shorts. These inappropriate choices can become opportunities for showing children how to compromise.

Jason's grandmother bought him a pair of swimming trunks with a sailboat appliqué. Not surprisingly, Jason wanted to wear his "boat pants" the next morning even though it was snowing out. "You can't go out with boat pants," his mother explained. "Boat pants are for summer when it's hot. I'll tell you what," she suggested, "We will put your boat pants on now and pretend it's summer. Then, before you go out, we will put on long pants."

When two-year-olds insist on wearing favorite clothes, they may show considerable interest in learning how to dress themselves. Being able to put on new shoes or a favorite dress is a clear demonstration of autonomy. Some two-year-olds, particularly if they have older siblings, adopt dressing skills as a sign of being grown-up. These children will spend long hours practicing. We watched Keisha, for example, struggle patiently for fifteen minutes to buckle a pair of sandals. When she stood

up, they were on the wrong feet. No matter, she sat down again and spent another fifteen minutes switching them around.

Two-year-olds who are intent on practicing dressing skills may even get in the habit of changing their clothes several times a day. This habit can be distressing to parents because the clothes that are removed are left all over the house, and the dresser where the child's clothes are kept usually looks as if a cyclone hit it. Frustrating as this behavior is, parents can console themselves with the thought that their child is already learning how to be independent in the important area of dressing.

Many parents find that their two-year-olds show little interest in learning how to dress themselves. These parents have often established a pattern in which dressing is a leisurely social occasion. It has been a time when the parents and children converse, play silly games, and sing songs. Parents need to recognize that children with this kind of experience are going to learn to dress themselves later than other children. The children resist dressing themselves because they enjoy both the social stimulation and the feeling of being waited upon. Their way of expressing autonomy is to insist that this pattern be continued.

Parents in this kind of situation will be most effective if they try to make learning how to dress a part of a social occasion as well. Peter's mother, for example, suggested that they take turns. "My turn with your socks," she said cheerfully as she put the socks on. "Now it's your turn to pull them up." She always engineered the sharing so that Peter finished the task. Kelly's mother used singing. As Kelly stuck her arms through the sleeves in her shirt, her mother sang, "This is the way Kelly puts on her shirt, puts on her shirt, puts on her shirt." Gradually Kelly assumed more and more responsibility for putting on her clothes, and her mother's job was reduced to singing.

Whether two-year-olds are primarily oriented toward dressing or undressing, they make a great deal of progress during this year. There still will be many things about dressing they do not understand or cannot accept, but this should come as no surprise. A family's rules governing the purchase, use, and care of clothing are very complicated. Two-year-olds start by focusing on what they can put on or take off their own bodies. Parents will find many opportunities to expand this limited vision, to show children how clothes proceed from the dirty clothes hamper through the washing and drying cycle to the appropriate dresser; how old clothes wear out and new ones are bought; how clothes become too small, too thin, or too stained. Learning the skills of dressing is just the beginning.

## Washing Up

When we arrived at Coretta's house, she was finishing a breakfast of French toast and syrup. "I wash my hands all by myself," she told her father as he helped her down from the high chair. "Cold water first," she told herself as she turned on the right hand faucet. After a good five minutes of hand scrubbing, Coretta's father suggested that her hands were clean and handed her a towel. Like most two-year-olds, Coretta enjoyed washing her hands as long as she could play in the water.

Brushing teeth is also a favorite activity for most two-year-olds. It is a new accomplishment that allows them to play with water and makes them feel grown-up. Squeezing the toothpaste is a great deal of fun and, if parents do not supervise carefully, a large portion of the tube gets used in a single brushing.

Unless parents mention the nasty term "hair wash," bath time is also great fun for two-year-olds. Any earlier fears of going down the drain have probably been conquered by now, and children enjoy splashing, pouring, making waves, and mixing the water with soap. A favorite activity is lining up toys on the side of the tub and making them dive in.

Hair washing is quite a different story. Most two-year-olds at some time or other have gotten soapy water in their eyes and have become very resistant to hair washing. Linn Su, for example, was basically a mild and pliable child who followed her parents' suggestions, but the sight of a shampoo bottle sent her into a frenzy. Hair-wash night was dreaded as much by her parents as it was by her, but finally her mother got an idea. She took Linn Su to the beauty parlor and let her watch several ladies getting their hair washed. That night Linn Su and her mother played beauty parlor. They sat Linn Su's doll on the edge of the bathtub, and Linn Su became the shampoo lady. "Stay still, and keep your head back, Doll," her mother commented. "Don't cry, Doll," her mother went on, "Linn Su won't let the soap get in your eyes." After a while Linn Su agreed to put a tiny bit of shampoo into her own hair, and her mother became the shampoo lady.

Several other techniques were used by parents to make hair washing less traumatic. Amy's mother used a sand pail to rinse her daughter's hair. Gregory's mother helped him keep his head back by making a wash cloth puppet do tricks while she rinsed his hair. Celestine's mother went into the shower with Celestine, and they took turns washing each other's hair.

Shampooing a doll's hair is an excellent way to desensitize children who are so terrified of hair washing that they will not let parents put the shampoo in their hair. A related technique is to encourage a two-year-old to put shampoo in a parent's hair. Still another idea is to let children watch themselves in a mirror while the shampoo is put on their hair. The white lather that appears gives them an interesting crown, and they may be intrigued by the effect.

The key to hair washing with two-year-olds is to find some procedure that relaxes your child. If children are relaxed in the shower, or when a pail of water is dumped over them in the bathtub, it will not be too difficult for them to learn to keep

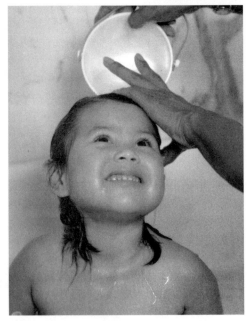

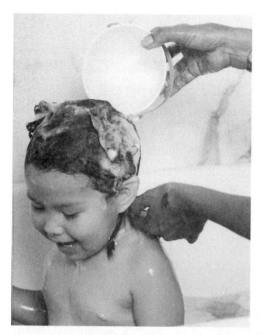

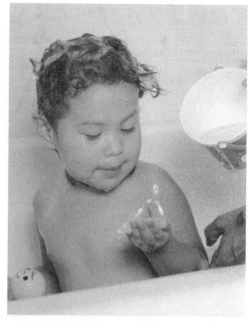

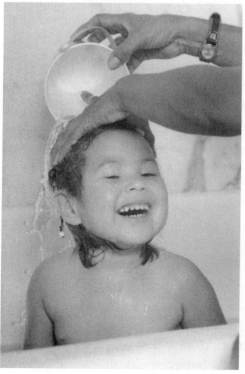

their eyes closed until all the soap is gone. If children can relax lying down in a few inches of water in the bathtub, or on a counter, the rinsing problem is solved. Learning to relax in a potentially frightening situation takes time. When children have developed a fear of hair washing, or of water in their eyes, parents need to realize that any technique will require patience on their part. Invariably, the children will one day be bursting with pride because they have learned to wash their hair without crying. A word of caution: Whether your child is playing in the bath or attempting to wash himself, never leave your child unattended. Two-year-olds have drowned in only an inch of water.

# TOILET LEARNING

Toilet learning is a major issue for parents of two-year-olds. While it may not make much difference to the children whether they learn to use the toilet at twenty-four or thirty-six months of age, this twelve-month span usually makes a big difference to parents. The messy diaper that was changed cheerfully during toddlerhood begins to produce frustration as the child approaches three, particularly if parents have selected a preschool that won't accept children in diapers. Unfortunately, just at the

time when parents feel pressured to toilet train their two-year-olds, their children may be at a stage where they want to stay in control. From a two-year-old's point of view, something that came out of their body belongs to them, and they shouldn't be told where to put it.

The parents we visited who approached toilet learning with moderate expectations handled this dilemma most easily. They actively urged their children to develop self-control, without worrying that toilet learning was fraught with symbolic significance. They did not assume that a few mistakes on their part would result in deep psychological trauma to their children. At the same time, these parents did not believe that toilet learning was as simple and mundane a matter as some psychologists claim. They anticipated that it would take a number of months, rather than a few days, to shape the child's behavior. In short, the parents

with moderate expectations adopted a common-sense philosophy where toilet learning was seen as a substantial but ordinary
challenge for two-year-olds.

Most of the parents we talked with were convinced that
toilet learning should be delayed until their children had sufficient neuromuscular coordination to control bowel and blad-
der functions. However, since it was not always easy to tell
when this point of maturation had been reached, parents were
a bit unsure about when to begin. Many of the parents had

started toilet learning, at least on a casual basis, between eighteen and twenty-four months. They invited their children into the bathroom as often as possible, showed them what was happening, and let them help flush the toilet. They encouraged their children to sit on the toilet themselves and in this way discovered if the child preferred a regular toilet, a potty chair, or a seat that fits on the regular toilet.

By the age of two, many children respond to this kind of consistent but low-key approach. Even if they are only interested in placing a doll on the toilet or flushing the toilet, it is a beginning. The next step is to help the children have some successful experiences while sitting on the toilet and to demonstrate to them that they can do what is expected. Ideally this step should not be initiated until it is clear that a child enjoys sitting on the toilet and feels relaxed. The more relaxed the child feels, the longer she will stay seated on the toilet, and the greater the likelihood that urination or elimination will occur. Parents need to feel relaxed as well, for their mood will be picked up by their children.

Grandparents, friends, and "experts" on toilet learning may be able to suggest some gimmicks for getting things started. For example, the faucet in the bathroom sink can be turned on and the child's attention directed to it. The sight and sound of running water causes some children to sympathetically urinate. Before taking a bath, a child can step into a tub of warm water, then get back out and go to the bathroom. The warm water induces urination, and many children first observe their ability to urinate when in the bathtub.

As a child's success experiences begin to occur with some regularity, parents may decide to start training in earnest. At this point, children can switch from regular diapers to pull up diapers. Parents recognize that toilet learning is difficult to complete when children are left in diapers. Children cannot remove the diapers easily in order to sit on the toilet. Pulling underpants up and down also takes some practice, but it paves the

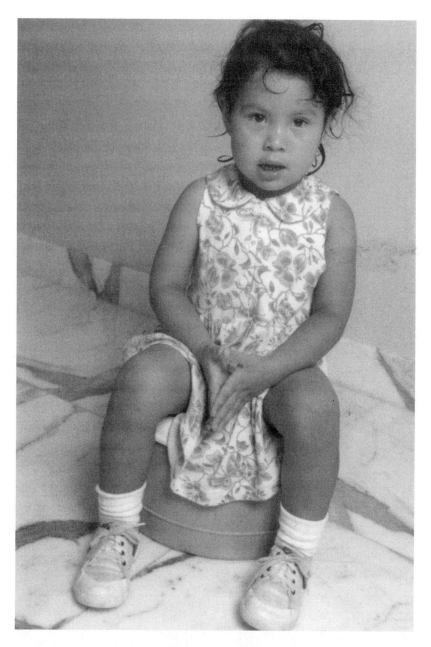

way to greater independence. In addition, children may have become accustomed to, perhaps even comfortable, going to the bathroom in their diapers. Putting them in underpants breaks this association.

CHAPTER 5

# *Helping Out*

~~~~~~~~~~~~~~~~~~~~~~~~~~~~~~~~~~~~~~~~

Kelly's grandmother had invited the family to brunch. "Do you suppose you could be finished with the housework in an hour and get over early?" Grandma asked. "I think so," Kelly's mother answered, "as long as Kelly doesn't decide that she would like to help."

Two-year-olds like Kelly enjoy helping out. They love to wipe off a counter, sweep the floor, wash the dishes, and water the plants. Parents usually appreciate their child's desire to be helpful. At the same time, parents realize that, despite good intentions, children's assistance can be a hindrance. We suggest playful strategies that parents can use to solicit help without violating their children's need to be the boss and to do things their own way.

## FOLLOWING DIRECTIONS

*Mother: "Andrew, let's go. It's time for school."*
*Andrew: "I don't want to go to school."*
*Mother: "You love school. Let's go."*
*Andrew: "I hate school."*
*Mother: "Okay, then you can stay home."*
*Andrew: "I don't want to stay home. I want to go to school!"*

This anecdote is not atypical. Regardless of the situation, two-year-olds like to be the boss and they don't like someone telling them what to do. But there are other reasons why two-year-olds rebel. Sometimes they are asked to do something they don't want to do. At other times the problem is making a transition. If they are having fun playing they don't want to stop, even if they could have more fun doing something else. Still an-

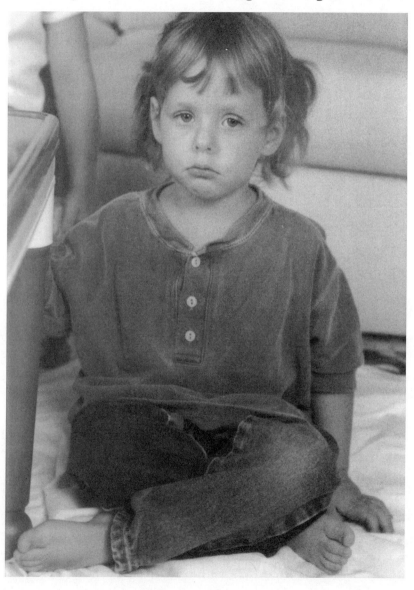

other reason for noncompliance is their parents' tone of voice. If the parent is up in arms, the children are likely to battle.

While two-year-olds don't like to do what they are told to do, they do like following directions. This is particularly true if the directions are presented as a challenge.

*Mother: "Andrew, do you suppose you could find my shoe? I may have left it under the sofa."*

*Andrew: "I found it."*

*Mother: "You are a very good finder. Now, can you find the pencil I dropped on the floor? Great, you found it, and I thought it was lost."*

This game went on for a long time and Andrew and his mother were having fun. It's easy to recognize why Andrew resisted going to school when he really loved it, but was perfectly willing to put down his toys and help his mother find lost things. In the finding game, Andrew is in control. His mother was challenging him to find the shoe. She wasn't making a demand.

Two-year-olds like Andrew enjoy the challenge of following a silly directive. At nursery school they enjoy playing Head, Shoulders, Knees, and Toes. At home they like to find Daddy's glasses and put them on his nose, or show a parent their elbow. On shopping trips they like to be given a special job to do. Marguerita, like most two-year-olds, loved to press the elevator button when she and her mother went shopping in the mall. One day when they were in a department store, Marguerita wanted to be the elevator operator. "Push the number one button," her mother suggested, "and take us down to the first floor." Understandably, Marguerita pushed the bottom button and they ended up in the basement. "What a silly button," her mother commented, "it was hiding in the wrong place."

As Marguerita's mother realized, two-year-olds can have trouble following directions even when they are trying very hard. It is particularly difficult to follow more than one direction at a time. Peter's father asked him to bring his shoes upstairs, put them in the closet, and then bring down his sneakers. Peter made off with the shoes but came down with nothing in his hands. "I told you to bring down your sneakers," his father reminded him.

Peter's father didn't realize that two-year-olds may have a problem remembering a string of directions. Following two or more directions is a learning process. Peter had no trouble bringing his Dad the newspaper, and was equally successful when he was asked to put the napkin on the place mat. "You are such a big helper," his father remarked and took time to give him a hug. It wasn't long before Peter was able to set the whole table with minimum directions from his parents.

Two-year-olds enjoy following directions when they know they can be successful. At the same time, and in the same way that they are turned off by a puzzle that is not challenging, or a puzzle that is too difficult, they resist following directions that are either too easy or too difficult. They may tire of "Give me five" if they are asked to do it too often, and they may resist doing up a seat belt if they can never get it to behave.

If we think about it, much of what a child learns at any age is related to following directions. Most adults learn a new computer skill best if someone is standing beside them telling them what to do. Once two-year-olds understand language, parents can use words to help them learn new things. Peter learned to open the door to the closet when his father told him to turn the knob and then pull. After her mother explained that first you put in your toes and then you pull hard, Celestine was able to put on her new boots.

# PICKING UP

The major issue concerning housework is picking up. Parents differ greatly in their expectations. Some parents expect children to be responsible for picking up their own toys from the age of eighteen months on; others think that four years old is about the right age. Most of the families we visited felt that two-year-olds should participate to some extent in picking up.

Looking more closely at the conflict over picking up, it appears that the real issue is the use of toys in certain parts of the house. Toys scattered in a child's bedroom are not too upsetting. It is the mess in the family room, or the clutter in the kitchen, that causes most of the trouble. Of course, children transport their toys to the "living" rooms of the house as soon as they begin to walk (or even crawl). But it seems that between the ages of two and three, many parents hope this situation will change.

One reason for expecting change is that the children are beginning to play independently in their own bedroom. Another reason is that a two-year-old can understand explanations. A third reason is that the patience of parents simply gives out. Parents get tired of the clutter and decide they have put up with it long enough.

In the strictest households we visited, parents tried to enforce the rule that children get out only one or two toys at a time. When they were finished playing with those toys they were supposed to put them back before getting out others. This rule was more a vision in the minds of parents than a reality. In most cases the rule led to continual conflict. Even children who enjoyed cleanup time at nursery school were not at all interested in picking up toys at home.

Most families aimed for one or two general cleanups a day. This practice was successful if parents helped. If they tried to force children to pick up on their own, a slowdown, or even a sit down, was likely. This suggests to us that two-year-old children do not really accept the need for picking up, but if it is part of a pleasant social experience, they are happy to participate.

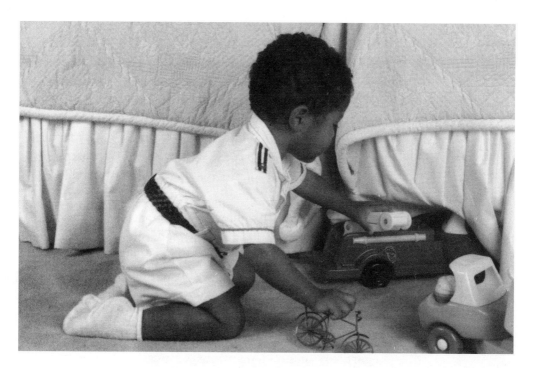

When parents help pick up, it also makes the activity like an adult job. Participating in an adult activity is much more likely to appeal to a two-year-old's sense of autonomy. Several families had provided toy boxes or baskets in the living room. In this way toys could be picked up without taking them to the bedroom. This idea makes picking up more convenient, and it also may make it more important in the eyes of a child. From a child's viewpoint, taking toys to the bedroom may seem almost insulting. These toys are precious possessions and they are being excluded from the important parts of the house.

Turning cleanup into a game encourages children to take part. "Let's park your trucks in the garage under your bed. Your dolls and stuffed animals are sleepy. Let's put them to bed. Here I go, throwing the ball into the basket. Now it's your turn." Don't be surprised, however, if children want to continue playing after all the toys are put away. Children are likely to feel that the cars have been in the garage long enough, that the dolls are ready to wake up, and basketball is a game that you should keep on playing. Putting toys away becomes an endless game.

The most easily understood reason for picking up is that it keeps toys from getting lost or misplaced. Two-year-olds readily understand this principle with individual toys. They enjoy finding the pieces and fitting them together. But when the toys are then piled in a toybox, the purpose for picking up becomes obscure.

A shallow cabinet on wheels with narrow shelves and a door is an especially good alternative. Opening and closing the door makes the cabinet an exciting container, while the shelves allow the child to find individual toys easily. For parents who are very intent on teaching a two-year-old to pick up, we would recommend building or buying such a cabinet and wheeling it to wherever the child plays most often.

Regardless of how ingenious or persistent parents are, most two-year-olds will continue to see picking up as a social activity. They will not be very interested in doing the job by themselves. Parents may think that a few weeks, or months, of picking up with the children will be sufficient to model this behavior. Our experience indicates, however, that it takes a much longer time for children to internalize the value of a tidy room. It is reasonable to introduce the idea of picking up at this age, but it is unrealistic to expect the lesson to be fully learned.

# CHAPTER 6

# *Keeping the Peace*

*Isabel and her mother were on the playground. Isabel had just learned to master the*
*slide and was intent on practicing this new skill.*

*"Just one more slide," her mother told her. "We have to go home and make dinner."*

*When Isabel finished her one more slide she was not ready to go home. "One more*
*slide," she insisted as she climbed up the steps of the slide.*

*Her mother caught her as she came down the slide. "We're going home right now. It's*
*time for dinner and that's that."*

*"I don't want dinner," Isabel insisted, "I want to go down the slide."*

*Her mother countered by picking her up and carrying her kicking and screaming off*
*the playground.*

Perhaps Isabel's mother could have avoided this conflict.
She could have been more matter of fact in telling Isabel it
was time to go home, and used playful techniques to make
going home enticing. Here's how the anecdote might have been
written.

*Isabel and her mother were on the playground. Isabel had just learned to master the*
*slide and was intent on practicing this new skill. "Quick, climb up the steps like*
*a monkey, and then go down the slide. You and I have something important to*
*do." Isabel's mother caught her "monkey" who squirmed out of her arms and*
*ran back to the steps. Her mother caught her again and swung her into the air.*
*"You are a wonderful monkey, but we have to go home now. We have something*
*important to do. We have to make dinner together. Do you want to set the table,*
*or would you rather make the lettuce salad?" By this time Isabel and her mother*
*had left the playground and were on their way back home.*

In this chapter, we suggest several ways of keeping the peace: avoiding conflicts before they happen, playful distraction, and nonpunitive ways of enforcing the rules.

# KNOWING YOUR TWO-YEAR-OLD

Every conflict between parent and child is a learning experience. Once parents can predict when a conflict is likely to take place, and analyze the reason a conflict took place, keeping the peace becomes a reasonable goal.

A first suggestion for parents is to think about their child's characteristic behaviors. Some children are easygoing most of the time, but are irritable and unreasonable when they are tired or hungry. Some children, on the other hand, can get so engrossed in play that they could go on forever without getting hungry or tired. Another difference between children is the sort of situation that is likely to produce a conflict. Some children are difficult to manage at home and perfect angels when they go on a visit. Other children are fun and easy when they're home and impossible to control when they're out. By recognizing the sorts of situations that are apt to create a battle of wills, parents can be more reasonable in their expectations and less frantic when things go wrong.

Another suggestion for parents is to take the point of view of a two-year-old. Two minutes is a very long time when they are waiting and a very short time when they are playing. Concepts like politeness and caution make little sense to a two-year-old. Why should you have to kiss a relative if you dislike kissing? Why do you have to hold your parent's hand when you know perfectly well how to cross a street?

Once parents understand their child's point of view, they are in a better position to negotiate. Coretta, who hated kisses, was allowed to shake hands with a visitor. Allison, who felt perfectly capable of crossing the street without holding her mother's hand, was asked to hold her mother's hand really tight so her mother would be safe.

A third suggestion is to recognize some typical two-year-old characteristics. Two-year-olds have difficulty staying still or keeping quiet. They are upset when they want to take their time and are forced to hurry, or want to hurry when their parents are taking too long. Two-year-olds want to be carried when they're frightened or tired, whether or not their parent is carrying a heavy package. When parents recognize what kinds of behaviors are typical of two-year-olds, they are able to accept some resistance without getting upset.

# AVOIDING CONFLICT

Eddie was sitting in an ice cream parlor with his older sister and parents. He put his hand on the table and began to finger his mother's spoon. She slapped his hand without looking down and continued arguing with her husband. Several minutes later Eddie fingered her spoon again. This time the mother picked up the spoon and hit him across the fingers. Just at that moment the waitress arrived with a tray full of ice cream sundaes. Eddie's mother stuck a spoon in the ice cream and told her son to go ahead and eat. Eddie stared at the spoon with frightened eyes and never touched the ice cream.

Eddie's mother was obviously upset. She wanted Eddie to sit quietly while she settled accounts with her husband. Unfortunately, the technique she used had a negative outcome that she did not anticipate. Knowing that Eddie did not like waiting in a restaurant, she might have found a way to keep him busy: a book, a toy, or perhaps even a snack. A little bit of planning could have avoided this conflict.

Andy was particularly fond of a pair of overalls with two

pockets that he had inherited from his older brother. Most of the time his mother was perfectly happy to wash them at night and let him wear them in the morning, but there were exceptions. Easter morning was one of those exceptions, and Andy's mother was not about to let him go to church in tattered overalls. The night before Easter, with the overalls still in the wash, she suggested to Andy that they go to his closet and choose an outfit for church. Andy took a while to decide between the blue pants and the green pants, but he finally made his decision.

Alese's mother found another way to handle a dressing problem. She was working in a job that required a great deal of travel. Her husband had no problem taking care of Alese except in the morning before school. No matter what choices Alese was offered, she wanted something different, and the something different she wanted was usually inappropriate. One day, before going on a trip, Alese's mother had an idea. She selected an appropriate outfit for every day she would be away. She carefully wrapped each outfit she selected in leftover Christmas paper. Alese loved opening her morning surprises, and there was no more hassling over clothes.

Although Andy and Alese's parents found different ways to avoid conflict, their strategies had something in common. Even though the children did not get exactly what they wanted, the strategies their parents used gave them a feeling of control.

Preparing a child for what is going to happen is another way of avoiding conflicts. Horatio had a dentist appointment and his mother anticipated a major battle. Two days before the appointment she read a story about a bear who visited the dentist. Then she acted out a pretend trip to the dentist with Horatio. She invented facsimiles of dental instruments. Horatio became the dentist, and she played the part of the patient. She engineered the play so that they acted out a sequence of events. First she pushed the button on the way up to the dentists office, walked over to an imaginary receptionist and told her her

name, sat down in a big chair, opened her mouth, and asked the dentist Horatio if her teeth were clean. At the end of the pretend visit, she asked the dentist Horatio to please give her a balloon. Her strategy worked, and Horatio made it through his visit to the real dentist without giving her a hard time.

Unfortunately, it is not possible to avoid every hassle by preparing a child ahead of time. On some occasions, two-year-old children actually become more difficult to live with if they are told what is coming. Anticipating a very exciting experience, they cannot wait; dreading an upcoming event, they stew about it. In general, though, two-year-olds are much more amenable to parental plans when they know about them a few hours, or perhaps a day, in advance. Parents who know their child's pattern can prepare themselves for the inevitable.

## Planning Ahead

Planning ahead is facilitated by setting up rules that two-year-olds can learn and follow. The daily routine then becomes predictable and children can act accordingly. Children as young as two years old are capable of obeying a rule if it is stated clearly and firmly. "No walking in the road." "No cookies in the morning." "Hitting is against the rules." Often, parents find that rule-setting is even more effective when the rules are stated in a more positive way. "You may go out as far as the sidewalk." "Remember to use your words." "Cookies are for your afternoon snack."

Two-year-olds usually learn these rules informally as different situations arise. In Frank and Constance's family, the parents reinforced rules by holding family meetings. Once a month the family gathered in the family room, where the twins drank milk from coffee cups and their mother served cinnamon rolls. The parents restated those rules the children were having trouble observing, and the whole family discussed special activities that Frank and Constance were allowed to do, such as mixing the orange juice, getting the newspaper, and operating the garage door opener. Frank and Constance's parents described holidays and other memorable events that would occur soon, and each member of the family was given a job. At Thanksgiving, for example, Frank was the roll man and Constance was the cranberry woman. Despite their tender age, Frank and Constance enjoyed these family meetings and listened attentively to the discussion.

Whether rules are presented casually or systematically it is best to apply them consistently. At the same time, situations are always changing, children are growing, and parents are developing new insights. Yesterday's rule may not be as good as today's idea. We visited one home in which the mother assured us that there were never exceptions to rules like, "No dessert unless you finish your meal," or "No playing with things in stores." This degree of consistency seems artificially rigid. It does not help children learn about compromise, which may be the rule in many real world settings.

## Distractions

An effective technique for keeping the peace is distraction. Parents can often avoid conflict with very young children by cheerfully removing them from troublesome situations. At other times, children can be given a substitute object to replace one that has been taken from them. As children grow older, however, they hold onto their ideas more tenaciously and it is harder to distract them. Some fast talking and imagination may be needed to make a distraction work. Zachary, for example, was going through a stage of refusing to drink his milk. One evening Zachary's father decided to try distracting him with a pretend game.

*Father: "Oh, I know what's wrong with this milk. It needs a little ketchup in it."*
*(Pretending to pour the ketchup in the milk.) "There now, I'm sure it will taste*
*good. Try it and see."*
*Zachary (grabbing the milk and taking a sip): "It tastes terrible!"*
*Father: "It does?" (Sounding incredulous.) "Oh, of course. I know what's missing.*
*Just a sprinkle of Meow Mix. Now I'm positive it will taste good."*
*Zachary (grabbing the milk and trying it again): "It tastes terrible, terrible!"*

Distraction is an excellent way to avoid conflict when the reason for a parental request is complicated and hard to explain. Two-year-old children have difficulty understanding why they should eat certain foods but not others, why they have to go to bed at a certain hour, or why they cannot take a friend's toy home with them. Using humor and imagination to distract a child in these situations puts off the conflict until a later day when perhaps the child will be better able to understand an explanation.

In Zachary's case, the distraction worked because it appealed to a two-year-old's sense of autonomy. Even though his father was only pretending to doctor the milk, Zachary enjoyed the opportunity to prove him wrong. Distraction also has definite limitations. Both parents and children have to be in the right mood. Parents need to feel fairly relaxed in order to be funny or imaginative, and children must have some flexibility in their position as well. Distraction does not work with a really serious conflict, or when there is not enough time to play games.

## No Contest

A final technique for avoiding conflict is to develop a very loose schedule in which children participate in the routines of their parents and parents participate in the routines of their children. When we arrived at Mary's house, she was standing at the door with a cold hot dog in her hand. "One for me and one for you," she sang to a bedraggled rag doll as she held the piece of hot dog up to its embroidered mouth. Mary's mother explained casually that the hot dog was Mary's breakfast. Mary always decides what she wants for breakfast and assists in its preparation.

After breakfast, Mary and her mother do the housework together. Because Mary's mother sets a slow pace, Mary is able

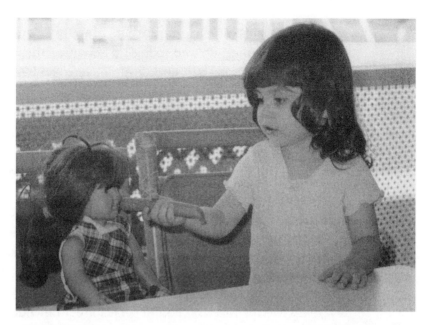

to join in. Mary plays with toys some of the time, but much of her play consists of helping or imitating her mother. We watched them clean a sliding glass door, Mary on one side and her mother on the other. At lunch time Mary set the table, which was another favorite activity. As she put the silverware around the table, her mother capitalized on the teaching opportunity, "Good, you remembered to take out three forks. One for Mommy, one for Daddy, and one for Mary."

# EXERCISING AUTHORITY

No matter how creative and proactive they are, eventually all parents are placed in a position where they must exercise authority. However, this is not necessarily a negative outcome. Conflict situations provide parents with an opportunity to establish sensible rules, to set limits, to teach values, and to help children make appropriate decisions. Daily routines that are most likely to induce conflict are also the source of some of the greatest pleasures in parenting. Many parents reported that shared cleaning-up and fixing-up activities, mealtime conversations, and before-bed-cuddle-time were the best parts of their day.

From our talks with different families about the kinds of concerns they have regarding routines, we can make two broad generalizations. First, the situations that bring about conflict reflect the value system of the family. Parents who are particularly concerned about nutrition are likely to have conflicts around food. Parents who emphasize the importance of sleep often have trouble over naps and bedtime. Parents who are concerned with teaching independence have more than the usual number of confrontations over self-help skills, such as dressing and toilet learning. Second, each family has a distinctive style for meeting conflict. Despite a bewildering variety of situations, there is a pattern of consistency in the way parents handle routine problems. Each family's style is a unique blend of strategies, some aimed at avoiding conflict and others aimed at enforcing compliance. The problem-solving techniques that parents use reflect their individual parenting styles.

## Talking it Over

The most practical technique for resolving a conflict is to talk about it. Words are very powerful for the two-year-old, and parents can often accomplish miracles by offering a serious explanation.

A well-meaning relative had given Kori her first box of lollipops. Although Kori's parents were certain that a well-balanced diet would keep Kori from developing a sweet tooth, they turned out to be wrong. Kori loved the lollipops and wanted to eat them for dinner. Her father thought this was a good opportunity to teach Kori about nutrition. He had no idea how much she would understand, but he gave Kori a brief explanation about the importance of protein. Kori forgot about the lollipops and went into the bedroom to get Raggedy Ann.

"Want your dinner, Raggedy? What do you want for dinner? No lollipops. No, no lollipops. You want yogurt? Yogurt has protein. Special K has protein."

Naturally, explanations do not work all the time. Sometimes a two-year-old isn't verbal enough to follow an explanation. Other times the child uses the "Let's talk about it" technique as manipulation. Brenan had gone to bed past his bedtime and was in that state parents always dread where he was simply too tired to go to sleep. After bringing two snacks and telling several bald-headed chicken stories, his father finally said, "Now it's really time to go to sleep, good night and no more calling." As soon as his father left the room, Brenan began to cry bitterly. This time his mother went into the room. "Okay, Brenan, stop crying," she stated firmly. "Let's talk about it," countered Brenan. "Let's talk about it in the living room."

Explaining rules to children actually encourages them to respond verbally. Children try to match their parents' reasons with reasons of their own. Although the children's arguments may be crude and far from logical, parents who genuinely believe in explaining things to children will find themselves compromising. Some of the time the children have a point.

## No Compromise Situation

When a two-year-old refuses to accept an explanation and a compromise solution is not possible, parents are placed in a position of invoking a stronger form of authority. Broadly speaking, they can try to induce children to go along with them by offering some kind of reward, or they can coerce the children by using some form of punishment.

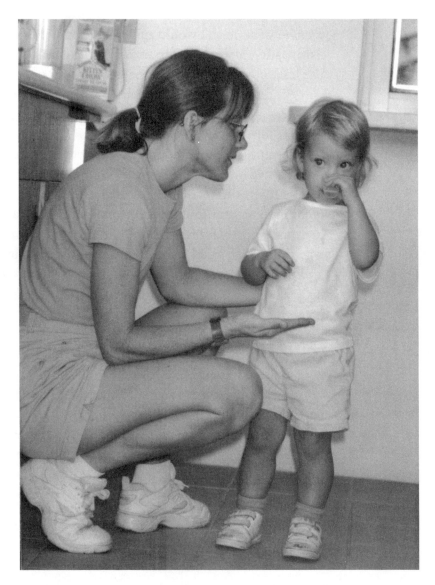

The parents with whom we talked used rewards extensively. In fact, all the techniques for avoiding conflict can be described as rewards. Children feel rewarded when they are included in future plans, offered a pleasant distraction, praised for following a rule, or allowed to share a common activity with parents. Rewards were also used on a systematic basis to overcome outstanding problems such as using the toilet, shopping in the grocery store, and taking medicine. However, parents are likely to use punishment rather than rewards in "no compromise" situations.

One explanation for this is that it is not always easy to think of an appropriate reward on the spur of the moment. Although most two-year-olds respond favorably to candy, many parents are against the idea of using food as a reward. Another reason may be that two-year-olds have difficulty understanding the conditionality of a reward. Lennie was told by his parents that, if he was a good boy and let the doctor see his tongue, Daddy would buy him a little car. Lennie was terrified in the doctor's office and had a full-blown temper tantrum. After the visit the real battle began. "I want car." "No." said Daddy, "you cried in the doctor's office."

"Car, want car," screamed Lennie, who felt that the very act of seeing the doctor justified the reward.

The kind of punishment mentioned most often by parents is criticism. Typically they criticize their child by saying, "I don't like that," or "I'm very mad at you." This kind of statement feels right to parents. It is emotionally honest. It is also a kind of explanation in that it goes beyond saying "Stop it," or "No." Parents are trying to explain how they feel. For the most part, children perceive this criticism as mild punishment. Parents regain their good humor after getting angry feelings off their chest, and children go back to their activities, not much worse for the experience.

Another form of mild punishment is to deprive children of some privilege. Parents reported that denying two-year-olds bedtime stories or favorite television programs just because they had been bad did not have much impact on the children. However, when the deprivation was logically connected to the misbehavior, the results were somewhat better. For example, when a two-year-old used a toy broom as a weapon and was subsequently not allowed to play with it for the rest of the day, the punishment helped her learn the rule.

Logical discipline, however, sometimes goes against common sense. The logical consequence of not taking a nap is being overly tired, but few parents are willing to let their children get in such a state. A logical punishment for being destructive or excessively restless is to restrict the playing space of the child, but several parents found that this approach made their children even more destructive and restless.

Isolation is another form of punishment that parents use. This technique is the most popular way to handle temper outbursts. Children are told to go to their room (or bed) until they can behave more acceptably. In Brandon's family, his father had actually built a fort in the family room. When Brandon was defiant, he was sent to his fort to play until all the bad feelings had gone away. Typically children who were isolated were allowed to decide when to come out. When they rejoined the family they were hugged and reassured. Parents were amazed at the transformation in their children, from being defiant to being happy and wanting to please.

Using isolation as a general discipline technique can have its drawbacks. At dinner one night, Mason expressed his own exhaustion by making the family miserable. He refused to eat his meat, kicked his sister, and finger painted on the table with his pudding. His father issued a firm order. "Go into your room and don't come out until you can eat your dinner." Mason returned in good spirits a few minutes later. After dinner, Mason was on his best behavior and even picked up this toys without being asked. Finally it was getting late and his mother suggested that they get ready for bed. Mason responded with genuine surprise. "I a good boy, I don't got to go in my room." Following this event, the family selected a back room rather than the bedroom as a cooling off place.

Here are some suggestions for using isolation as a disciplinary technique:

 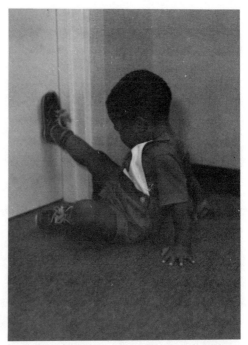

1. Use a comfortable chair in a family or living room as an isolation spot. (Using a bedroom is never a good idea.)
2. Introduce your child to the isolation spot when she is in a happy mood.
3. Show your child what the isolation spot is for by demonstrating its use with a teddy. "Teddy, you need to sit in the sweetening chair. When you are sweet and happy then you can come back to play."
4. Use a matter of fact voice and not an angry voice when you send your child to the sweetening chair.
5. Use the sweetening chair as your last resort.

While the sweetening chair often works well when your child has a tantrum, it is not always practical or appropriate.

1. If you know your child is having a tantrum because he's tired, hungry, or doesn't feel well, take care of the problem and not the tantrum.

 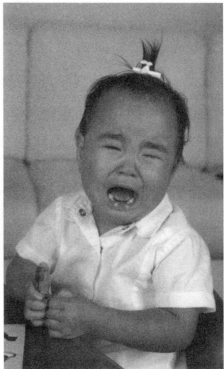

2. If your child has a tantrum out of the house, pick her up and announce firmly that she has to go home to the sweetening chair.

3. If your child refuses to go in the isolation spot, walk out of the room. (If your child can't be isolated then isolate yourself.)

4. No matter how tempting it is, do not yell or use physical punishment. As a role model for your child, you don't want to send out the wrong message.

# SECTION III

# MAKING
# CONNECTIONS

Allison and her grandfather were going through the family album starting from the back and moving to the front. Allison had no trouble recognizing the recent photos. First, she would look for her own photo, then she would name other members of the family. With the help of her grandfather, she would talk about what was happening in the photo. As they went from back to front, Allison became less interested. "Here you are when you were a baby," Grandpa pointed out. Allison was highly insulted. "I am not a baby. I'm a big girl."

In this section, we focus on the different ways that two-year-olds make connections with their world. They are developing a sense of self: what they look like, what they want, what belongs to them, and what they can do. Their language skills are developing in leaps and bounds. They can use words to express their needs, they understand much of the language they hear, and they are beginning to participate in back and forth conversation. They are also expanding their horizons, relating

with ease to other members of the family, to familiar adults, older children, and children their own age.

Two-year-olds experience rapid intellectual growth and emotional change. A major outcome of this growth is a new capacity to recognize themselves as separate individuals. Children become increasingly aware of their power to affect other people, especially parents, and they develop a distinctive style for social interaction. At the same time, they soak up new information and begin to realize the vastness of the world. Their vision of time and space, of life itself, expands tremendously. We will discuss the emerging world view of two-year-olds in terms of these two perspectives, a new sense of self and the making of new discoveries.

# CHAPTER 7

# Developing a Sense of Self

~~~~~~~~~~~~~~~~~~~~~~~~~~~~~~~

"**M**e want a piggyback," Allison insisted. "You don't say me want, you say, I want," her father explained. "But me wants a piggyback," countered Allison, putting extra stress on the "me."

Although two-year-olds learn to say "me" before they learn to say "I," their sense of self is well established. They recognize that they are separate from other people, that they have wants, needs, and good and bad feelings. A two-year-old can say "That book made me sad," "I am mad at you," or "I am scared of big bad dogs and spiders."

In this chapter, we talk about three manifestations of a sense of self: Self Recognition, Self Assertion, and Mixed Feelings. The acquisition of a sense of self is a critical component of a two-year-old's development. It is a prerequisite for taking responsibility for what you do and what you do not do.

## SELF-RECOGNITION

Tania was standing in front of the mirror wearing a new outfit that her aunt had bought her. "Come see, now come see," she called to her Mom. "Look, Mom, me in the mirror and me wearing my new dress."

By the age of two, most children can recognize their own image in a mirror and even their own photograph. They already have discovered, or are on the verge of discovering, their gender identity, and they generally are aware that human bodies consist of standard parts. In short, the children have a superficial, but stable, sense of their physical selves.

This sense of physical self does not exist in a vacuum. It is embedded in a larger environment of material things. Like other people, two-year-olds support their sense of identity by laying claim to this larger world. Being less sure of themselves, their possessiveness is more rigid and shrill. "That's mine," becomes a pronouncement with virtually no limits. Two-year-olds are possessive about their toys, their clothes, their house, and even their parents.

For a two-year-old, possessions are a way of extending a primitive sense of self. They provide stability rather than status. Several parents told us their children reacted negatively when the family car was traded in for a new one. The new car was fancier, but the old car was familiar. Moving to a new house, or even changing the furniture in the old house, is upsetting to some children. "I don't want you to take down my crib," Matthew insisted, even though he hadn't slept in his crib for months. "I don't want new shoes," Heather screamed, holding on desperately to the old shoes that she had outgrown.

One sign of a growing awareness of self is an emerging ability to express preferences. Children go beyond the immediate feeling of "I want" or "I don't want" and focus on "I like" or "I don't like." "I want that," Kori said to her Nana as she pointed to some iced coffee. "You won't like it," Nana explained. "It has a bitter taste." "I want to try that," Kori insisted a little more firmly. "Okay, try it," Nana agreed, "but take a little taste." Kori tried it. "I don't like Nana's coffee. I like Daddy's tea better."

Another sign of increased self-awareness is the growing ability of two-year-olds to talk about emotions. "It's a beautiful day," Zachary joyfully exclaimed as he and his mother chased a butterfly across the backyard. "I swinging, I swinging, I swinging, I so happy swinging," sang Wendy as she swung higher and

higher at the park. On the negative side, Daren let his father know how he felt about not being allowed to play with the toaster. "I hate you bad," he shouted emphatically. Jodi ran into her mother's room after watching a scary television show. "Mommy, that TV makes my tummy shake."

Two-year-olds are not only more articulate about their own feelings, they show greater sensitivity toward the feelings of others. When Allison accidentally broke a vase, she asked her mother plaintively, "Are you sad?" Isabel, who was just gaining enough control to use the toilet, greeted her mother at the door. "Feel my pants, Mommy. Are you happy?"

The self-awareness of two-year-olds comes out, above all, in the form of self-assertion. Assertive techniques include screaming, arguing, rationalizing, threatening, ordering, teasing, whining, hitting, kissing, hugging, making cute faces, and many others. Although some of these assertive techniques appear to be negative developments, they indicate social growth. Children from two to three concentrate on exploring the social environment, just as they focused earlier on the physical environment. The outcome of these explorations is a new repertoire of social skills.

A critical task for two-year-olds is learning when and how to use their new social skills. It is a problem of discrimination. Each technique has its place and is acceptable at times. The fact that parents respond differently in different situations makes it more difficult for children to learn appropriate behavior. In reality, social interaction is very complicated. It is not governed by a set of straightforward, simplistic rules.

For children who have just turned two, the most prominent technique for self-assertion is likely to be a defiant "no." Children discover that a "no" has power, and they use it at every opportunity.

*Mother: "Trevor, would you like to come to the drugstore with Daddy and me?"*
*Trevor: "No, don't wanna."*
*Mother: "You can pick out a birthday card to send to Pop-Pop."*
*Trevor: "No, don't wanna."*
*Mother: "Okay, then stay here with Jeffrey."*
*Trevor (bursting into tears): "Me go drugstore, Mommy, Daddy."*

Verbal forms of resistance become more subtle as the language ability of a two-year-old increases. Kori, for example, developed a string of imaginary characters who provided a ready-made excuse for resisting parental requests. "Would you like to help me put away your toys so that we'll be ready to go out when Daddy comes?" her mother asked. "No, I can't," Kori explained. "I have to look after Aki and her sisters and all the little babies." Amy, who discovered that she got special consideration because of a headache, started to develop stomach aches, leg aches, and back aches. Even peas were refused at dinner because "they hurt my mouth."

Conversely, two-year-olds develop positive techniques for manipulating parents. A please, a hug, a kiss, or a little flattery go a long way toward keeping parents "in line." Heather, for example, gave her father lots of hugs and kisses when he did things her way. When her father "misbehaved," she let him give her a good night kiss and then wiped it away with her sheet. Jeannette varied her technique to fit the situation. When she wanted candy from Grandma, she asked in a polite voice, "Please, Baba, candy." When she wanted a story from Daddy, she cuddled up on his lap and gave him a hug. A particularly effective strategy that some two-year-olds learn is "I'm sorry." Shawn had been playing with the water pump, although he knew full well that it was off limits. Just as his mother was about to scold him, Shawn looked up with a most innocent expression. "I sorry. You angry, Mommy?"

Two-year-olds practice new social skills just like any other new skill they develop. It would be incorrect, however, to assume that children are only involved in testing their ability to manipulate parents. When two-year-old children assert themselves, regardless of the technique, there usually is some genuine emotion involved.

Nicole's family told us they could not stand Nicole's incessant whining. Sure enough, as soon as we got to the house, Nicole began whining for a cookie. Her mother explained that she could not have a cookie because it was too close to lunch. Nicole continued to whine. Finally her mother could not hold out any more and gave Nicole a piece of cookie.

In this particular incident it was quite clear that Nicole's mother had reinforced the whining behavior. Nicole had learned from this incident, and probably from a lot more like it, that if your first whine does not produce the desired result, you had better whine louder and longer.

This example suggests that parents should not give in to whining. Such a rule, however, would overlook the fact that children whine when they are sad. Nicole was genuinely unhappy because she could not understand the reason for prohibiting cookies before lunch. In this instance, it would have been better for Nicole's mother to resist her request, but what if Nicole had been whining for some nutritious snack or because another child had taken away her toy? In these cases, many parents would decide that a child's unhappy feelings outweighed the manipulative aspects of whining. The parents might ask the children to make their requests in a different tone of voice, but they would not deny the requests because of whining.

# SELF-ASSERTION

Temper tantrums are an even more disconcerting form of self-assertion. Timothy's mother told us about a recent tantrum that had occurred at a park. Like many two-year-olds, Timothy loved exploring the playground equipment at parks. As a special treat, they had stopped at a new park on their way downtown. After fifteen or twenty minutes, his mother said it was time to leave and go shopping. His response was, "I don't wanna." When she took his hand, he suddenly pulled away, threw himself on the ground, and started to scream. "That tantrum really wasn't too bad," Timothy's mother reported. "Nobody else was near us, so I didn't feel embarrassed. I ignored Timothy's screaming, just picked him up and put him in the car. But when he pulls that kind of trick in a grocery store or restaurant, I don't know what to do."

As in Nicole's whining, there was both manipulation and genuine emotion in Timothy's behavior. He had learned from previous experience that he sometimes got his way by screaming. At the same time, he was genuinely angry because he could not understand the need to leave the park. Again, we have selected an example in which most parents would not respond to the temper tantrum. But what if Timothy had lost his temper because he could not complete a puzzle or because his ice cream cone had fallen on the ground? In such situations, many parents would respond to the child's expression of frustration and rage. They would offer to help with the puzzle or they would buy another ice cream cone. Each situation is different. Sometimes we refuse to be manipulated, sometimes we respond to the child's feelings, and sometimes we search for a compromise. There are no standard answers.

# MIXED FEELINGS

Each two-year-old blends different social skills into a personal style. Some children excel in being argumentative and defiant. Some are especially good at manipulating parents with hugs and kisses. Some make excuses and invent imaginary scapegoats. Some are whiners. All two-year-olds struggle with feelings of ambivalence about growing up.

"Now I am a big boy." Matthew told his mother as he pulled on a new pair of underpants. "Now I am a baby," he announced later as his naptime diaper was put on. The transition from babyhood to childhood is not accomplished without detours and backtracking. One moment the two-year-old refuses his father's hand as he mounts a flight of stairs or walks along a busy street. A moment later he is afraid of stepping over a crack in the sidewalk and asks his father to carry him. Two-year-olds want to do things for themselves but at the same time find it difficult to give up the protective environment of babyhood.

The brunt of this ambivalence is directed toward parents. It is not unusual to see a complete change in children's behavior when parents are not around. Parents recounted similar stories about first visits with relatives: the children acted like perfect angels, no hassles, no temper tantrums, and no defiance. From the moment the children got home, however, the spell of good behavior came to an abrupt halt. Parents described their children as being downright stubborn, reverting to babyish behavior, whining, asking to be carried, and even demanding a bottle. "Grandma just spoiled her rotten," one mother complained.

Although Grandma may have broad shoulders, it is probably not accurate to describe this reversion to babyishness as the result of spoiling. More likely the two-year-old is demonstrating a normal reaction to a temporary loss of home. Being on their best behavior with relatives and coping with a new environment is a strain for two-year-olds. When they return home, they feel secure enough to release pent-up feelings of ambivalence and to abandon their grown-up posture. Two-year-olds look forward, however, to outings with adults other than their parents and are likely to develop special relationships with grandparents, aunts, uncles, and teachers. Despite these expanding social horizons, parents continue to serve as the base of security for the two-year-old. Two-year-olds may have a marvelous time exploring new relationships but, in an emotional sense, they do not stray far from home.

# CHAPTER 8

# *Making Friends*

~~~~~~~~~~~~~~~~~~~~~~~~~~~~~~~~~~~~~~~~~~~~~~~~~~~~~~

Eight-year-old Ina came into the house angry and sobbing. "I hate Allison and I'm never going to play with her in my whole life and she's not my friend." Kelly, her two-year-old sister, looked surprised, "You don't like to play?"

A friend for a two-year-old is somebody you play with. Although two-year-olds do have special children that they love to play with, it is the playing that is important to them, and not the special attributes or behaviors of their playmate.

In this chapter we describe ways two-year-olds play with other children: with a same age peer, with one or two older children, and with a group of children in a nursery school or preschool.

## PLAYING WITH A FRIEND

When children play with their same-age peers, the play sessions are usually less smooth than they are with older children. One of the big bugaboos is sharing toys. Two-year-olds have just gotten a firm handle on the concept of possessions. They recognize that all members of the family have certain things that belong just to them. These facts frequently are reflected in the language of two-year-olds: "your briefcase," "my teddy bear," "Daddy's keys."

Being told to share possessions is a puzzling kind of request. Why do I have to share something if it really belongs to

me? Parents often urge their children to share because other children have shared with them. But how often is this true? From a two-year-old's perspective, other children frequently do not share, and they give every indication of wanting to keep the toys they are playing with. As adults, we know that a borrowed toy eventually will be returned to its original owner, but how do two-year-olds know that a toy still belongs to them if they agree to share it? The idea that possession is nine-tenths of the law must seem a very compelling argument to a young child.

Here again, we see the difference between only children and those with siblings. In a family with several children it is common to consider many of the toys as joint property. This gives the children more experience in sharing, and they are therefore more likely to share their toys with friends. The difference is only one of degree, however. In almost every family there are special toys that are the exclusive property of individual children. Brothers and sisters are not allowed to play with these special toys unless they have the owner's specific permission. When we visited Kyle, who was two and a half, he grudgingly allowed his sister to play with several of the toys in his room, but he would not let her sit on his firetruck.

Between the ages of two and three, many children learn to share their toys with certain friends in certain circumstances. However, it is not unusual for possessiveness to actually increase during this year. As children have more contact with peers, their reaction may be to guard their own possessions even more closely and to covet the possessions of others. Being able to share represents a feeling of trust, and it takes some children longer to extend this trust to their peers. Again it should be emphasized that every situation is different. Children's attitudes toward sharing are affected by whose home they are in, how long they have known the other child, the personality and age of the other child, and what toy is at issue.

Even when children have progressed to the point of sharing their toys, it often happens that the toy being requested is not a toy they are willing to share. Kori discussed this dilemma with her mother in a tearful conversation.

*Kori: "I don't want Jason to take my Snoopy. Jason play with my Snoopy too long.*
    *Jason can play with my harmonica."*
*Mother: "Yes, that's a good idea. You can bring Jason your harmonica."*
*Kori: "Jason don't want my harmonica. Jason can play with my bubbles."*
*Mother: "That's a fine idea."*
*Kori: "Jason don't want my bubbles. I don't want to share Snoopy. I can share*
    *Snoopy with Molly. Molly gives my toys back."*

As children turn three, they are more likely to demonstrate selective selfishness. Whether or not they agree to share depends on how much they like the person who wants to borrow. Andy did not like the twins who lived next door. Before his birthday party he told his mother that Mason couldn't eat his cake and Melinda couldn't swim in his pool.

Most parents of two-year-olds faced the problem of teaching their children to share. The rule most frequently used by parents is that whoever got a toy first had the right to play with it. This rule is crude, but it does communicate that grabbing a toy out of someone else's hand is wrong.

Sooner or later most parents try to explain why it is not nice to grab a toy. These explanations generally don't make much of an impression, judging from the dull look they inspire on a child's face. A two-year-old needs a concrete verbal formulation to understand the significance of the explanation.

Mary's mother seemed to have hit on a good idea. When a fight broke out over a toy she tried to find out who the trespasser was by referring to him as the grouch. "Who's the grouch now, Beverly? You're the grouch. Willie already had the cement mixer. Come on, grouch. Let's find you another toy." The children soon learned how the identity of the grouch was determined and that everyone was the grouch at one time or another. The verbal ritual of being labeled the grouch communicated, in a nonpunitive way, a basic rule of sharing.

Mary's mother had introduced another verbal formula that facilitated sharing at an early age. At the dinner table, food often was divided and distributed by saying, "One for Mary, one for Mommy, and one for Daddy." This formula was repeated in diverse settings, such as rolling a ball back and forth and saying, "One for Mommy . . . one for Mary." By the age of

two, Mary had shown interest in dividing her toys among her friends in the same way. The magic of counting helped her overcome the tendency to hoard possessions.

Matthew's mother suggested another technique. Many families allow children to take one toy along when they go visiting. This toy can be used in the car and also at a friend's house. Matthew's mother reversed the idea. She taught Matthew to choose one of his toys to share with his friend. In this way, Matthew was able to initiate the sharing by offering a toy to the host child, rather than the usual procedure of waiting for the largess of the host to materialize. Imagine how much less threatened host children must feel when their guest immediately gives them a new toy to play with. The idea is comparable to bringing flowers or wine when invited to dinner, a token of gratitude in advance.

CHAPTER 9

# Relating to Siblings

~~~~~~~~~~~~~~~~~~~~~~~~~~~~~~~~~~

*Allison sat down in the chair beside her father. "No fair," her brother shouted. "It's my turn to sit by daddy." "My turn," shouted Allison, holding on to the table. "Oh, let her sit there," her mother intervened. "She's a baby." "Baby, baby," Zachary shouted as he pushed his sister off the chair.*

Sibling rivalry goes with the territory when families have more than one child. Whether two-year-olds have an older or younger sibling, or their mother is having a new baby, they are likely to feel jealous. Even older children—especially older children—vie for the attention of their parents.

## EXPECTING A NEW SIBLING

Parents who have developed a close relationship with their first child are usually quite concerned when a new baby is expected. Will their two-year-old feel angry about the new baby? Will he exhibit symptoms of sibling rivalry like anger, jealousy, pouting, purposeful naughtiness, demanding behavior, and/or regression? Although some degree of sibling rivalry is inevitable, there are many strategies parents can use to help their two-year-old accept the fact that he won't be the baby in the house.

## *Before the Baby Is Born*

- When the baby is active enough, give your two-year-old an opportunity to feel your belly. Make sure to say "Feel the baby stretching," or "Feel the baby moving." Two-year-olds may not like the idea of a baby kicking their Mommy.
- Go through the baby book and show your two-year-old the pictures of when she was a baby. Talk about how she could not sit or walk or even feed herself.
- Sort through your two-year-old's baby clothes. Talk about how little he was when he was a baby. Help him choose the clothes that will fit the new baby soon after birth. Your two-year-old will get a feeling for how little the baby will be.
- Talk to your two-year-old about all the things the baby will be using: a crib, a carriage, a Snuggly, and perhaps a cradle. Don't be surprised if your two-year-old wants to try things out.
- Help your two-year-old take care of a baby doll. Introduce the idea slowly that babies need lots of time and care. Let her give her doll a bath in the new baby's tub. This is a good

time to talk about how gentle you have to be with a new baby.

- Let your two-year-old take part in your exercises. This time together gives you a chance to talk in a casual way about your new baby's birth.
- You and your two-year-old can make something together for the new baby. Choose something simple and easy to complete, like a quiet sign or a picture to go over the crib.
- Teach your two-year-old a lullaby to sing to the new baby. This will help him understand that he will be an important helper when the new baby is born.
- You and your two-year-old can plan the new baby's room together. Then take her on a shopping trip to buy some items for the new baby.
- Give your two-year-old a turn rocking in your arms in the new baby's rocking chair. Talk about how sometimes it's fun to be a big brother and sometimes it's fun to pretend to be a baby.
- Buy something for the two-year-old that connotes getting bigger and more grown-up, like crayons, a riding toy, or a breakable knickknack.

- If you are planning to breast-feed, invite a friend over who is breast feeding her baby. Your two-year-old will adjust more easily if she knows what to expect.
- In preparation for the baby's homecoming, let your two-year-old choose the outfit that the baby will wear home from the hospital. Your two-year-old will enjoy discovering how his baby looks in the clothes he selected.
- Drive to the hospital with your two-year-old. She will make a better adjustment to your going to the hospital if she knows where you are going to be.

## When the Baby is Born

Several weeks before the baby is due, begin to discuss the fact that soon Mommy and Daddy will be going to the hospital to bring the new baby home. Tell your two-year-old who will be coming to take care of him, that his daily routine will stay the same, and describe the special things he will be doing while Mommy is in the hospital. If your two-year-old is staying at a relative's house, let him be involved in packing his suitcase for the trip. Also, let him help you pack your suitcase. It will help him understand that you won't be away for long.

- Bring a Polaroid camera to the hospital so you can send a picture of the new baby home with Daddy.
- If your two-year-old enjoys phone conversations, call her from the hospital to tell her about the new baby.
- Have a special big sister or big brother present ready to give your two-year-old when the baby comes home. This may be a special baby doll for your two-year-old to take care of.
- Explain in advance the rules for holding the new baby. The rules may be that you have to be sitting in a chair, that Mommy or Daddy have to stand in front of you, and that the baby goes back to Mommy if he starts to cry.

- Have a homecoming party for the new baby. Since the baby is not old enough to eat birthday cake, your two-year-old will have to eat it for him.
- Read stories with your two-year-old about being a big sister or big brother. Choose books that will help your two-year-old cope with feelings of jealousy.

## *Adjusting to a New Baby*

Many two-year-olds seem to adjust quite easily when brother or sister first arrives home. They feel grown-up when they sort the baby's laundry, bring in a diaper, or find the baby's pacifier. (Many of the children are just mastering the toilet and are pleased when the baby messes.) When not helping Mommy or Daddy take care of the baby, two-year-olds are likely to tend their own dolls and stuffed animals. Dolls that have spent months in the bottom of a toy chest are resurrected and pressed into service.

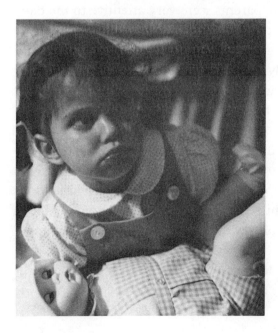
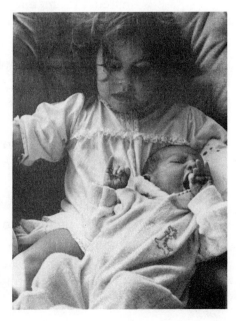

This honeymoon period may not last long. After a while, two-year-olds recognize that a new baby gets a special kind of attention. Adults are constantly vying for a chance to hold the baby, and the baby's every move is admired from all sides. Just when the parents have relaxed their fear of sibling rivalry the dreaded symptoms appear. Alesha's mother's account is fairly typical. "At first when the baby was born everything was peaches and cream, but just recently I'm seeing signs of jealousy. As soon as I begin to breast-feed the baby, Alesha starts with, 'I got to go potty, hurry up!'" In contrast to Alesha, Nicholas was forthright about his feelings toward his brother. "I don't like my brother," he informed his parents, "because you are always holding him." When Nicholas's mother sang to the baby "You Are So Beautiful," Nicholas voiced his protest. "Sing that song to me. Don't sing that to my brother."

In some cases, parents may be able to modify or tone down the special attention a new baby receives. Brandon's parents, for example, discovered that Brandon was jealous of the way they took care of the baby at night. Brandon and the baby shared a room, and the parents were very attentive to the baby whenever he cried out. Brandon tried crying out too, but he didn't get the same kind of attention. This source of jealousy was removed by simply moving the baby to another room. After that, Brandon slept through the night. Aaron's mother taught him to help with the baby's massage instead of pushing the baby "accidentally."

Another way to help two-year-olds cope with their jealousy is to allow them to participate in intimate interaction with the baby. Gregory's mother showed him how he could hold his baby sister's hand while she was drinking her bottle. Mary's mother taught her to play with the baby's feet instead of investigating his face.

While sibling rivalry may be an ever-present problem, two-year-olds, like adults, can be captivated by a cooing, smiling baby. Furthermore, two-year-olds have a natural ability to entertain babies. We observed several children playing with baby brothers and sisters in a crib or playpen. In these places, the usual relationships were reversed. The two-year-old took the lead in interacting with the baby and became the prime object of the baby's attention, while the parents watched from the sidelines.

Finally, parents can try to communicate to their two-year-olds that there are advantages in being the most grown-up child in a family. Mary's mother, for example, reminded Mary that she could move around, run, and jump, while the baby just had to lie on his back. Mary could drink from a cup and could even choose what to eat, while the baby always had to eat the same thing. The most dramatic way to demonstrate this idea is to take the two-year-old on a special outing without the baby. The outing can be very simple because the idea of having special time is more important than the activity. One of Brandon's favorite activities, for example, was to go around the corner and have breakfast with his mother.

# KEEPING UP WITH OLDER SIBLINGS

Parents are also concerned about the feelings of jealousy between two-year-olds and older siblings. The two-year-olds try to emulate their older brothers and sisters. They feel able to do the same things, and they expect the same privileges. Parents find themselves, on the one hand, encouraging their two-year-olds to develop new skills, but on the other hand trying to convince them that equal treatment is not always possible. In dealing with the older siblings, parents are caught in a similar dilemma. They want to support the rights of the older children, but at the same time they want them to be kind and generous with their younger sibling.

A two-year-old's feelings of sibling rivalry may be expressed in exaggerated "me too" behavior. Willie, who was just barely two, was watching his older sister Suzanne chewing gum. Willie didn't really know what gum was and was quite happy with the wrapper Suzanne gave him. He popped the wrapper in his mouth and started chewing. Apparently it didn't taste very good and the family giggled at his expression of surprise and disgust. However, Willie's demands for similar treatment continued, and after a while they stopped being funny. When Suzanne was given penicillin for an ear infection, Willie wanted his penicillin, too. When Suzanne put on a yellow dress for Sunday School, Willie cried bitterly until his mother let him wear a dress.

Another common way of expressing rivalry is learning how to tease. Christopher, the youngest of three children, was a master of this strategy. While we were visiting, he knocked down his sister's block building in a quick commando raid. Next he ran into the bedroom to retrieve and then hide his brother's favorite stuffed dog.

Still another way two-year-olds attempt to protect their turf is to demand more attention from their parents. When Jodi's older sister was showing her kindergarten papers, Jodi kept tugging at her mother's skirt and insisting, "I have something to tell you." Nicole's strategy was to appeal to her mother's sympathies. "Little Nicole is very sad because you won't pick me up. Little Nicole is a baby." Abdul had decided that if he couldn't get his fair share of attention by being good, he would certainly get it by being bad. As soon as his father began playing with his older brother, he deliberately engaged in every bothersome activity he could think of.

If all other tactics are ineffective, two-year-olds may directly attack their older siblings. They may break a brother's or sister's treasured possession. They may echo back the taunts of older children: "I don't like you. I won't even play with you. I won't be your friend." They may resort to biting, scratching, pinching, or throwing things.

Between two and three years of age, a child's confrontations with older siblings are likely to intensify. Battles over possessions, privileges, and status in the family are continually rocking the household. From the point of view of parents, the most ridiculous things can create the biggest ruckus. Who is

going to sit in the brown chair in front of the television set? Who gets the rose on the icing of the birthday cake? Who turns the pages in the *Goodnight Moon* story book?

Parents naturally feel badly about these signs of sibling rivalry, and they inevitably blame themselves. Although this kind of self-blame is understandable, it certainly is not warranted. Actually, sibling rivalry is a good sign. It shows that children value the time and attention of their parents. We found, in fact, that sibling rivalry was most intense in child-oriented families. In families where parents were punitive or aloof, siblings had much less reason to compete with each other.

# WAYS OF RESPONDING TO SIBLING RIVALRY

Every family develops its own philosophy for handling the rivalry between two-year-olds and older siblings. Some parents feel that it is their responsibility to intervene in sibling fights and teach the children how to get along. Timothy's mother, for example, was a firm believer in settling differences by talking about them. "If I stand there and let them fight, I am actually condoning fighting. I am saying to them, 'Go ahead, fight it out, might makes right.' No, sir. I tell my children that we talk over problems with our mouths, not our fists, and, you know, even my two-year-old understands." When Timothy's sister borrowed his security blanket to cover her doll, Timothy came running into the room tumbling over his words, "Allison, my blanket. Allison took it, my blanket. Talk about it, Mommy."

Other families adopt a hands-off policy toward sibling rivalry. They believe that children will resolve their differences sooner or later if left alone. Christopher's father put it this way: "You can't pull kids apart every time they get into a fight. It's a tough world out there, and they have to learn to stand up for themselves. I tell my wife, 'Don't ever pull the kids apart unless you see blood.'"

In most cases, families find themselves somewhere between these extremes. They try to diffuse sibling rivalry but without actually intervening and requiring the children to behave in a certain way. One family, for example, tried to turn potential conflicts into playful situations. When Abdul insisted that his cookie was smaller than Angeline's, their mother responded by saying that she would feed Abdul's cookie some vitamins so that it would grow bigger. Although this kind of humor may go over the children's heads, the cheerful parental tone is catching.

Most families also make a conscious effort to communicate to their children that they are equally loved. One approach with young children is to establish a special time for each child to interact with parents. This is a common practice at bedtime. The children go to bed at different times and each one gets a story or some form of special attention before they go to sleep. We visited one family who had carried this idea much further and felt happy with it. Peter, the two-year-old, had his time with mother during a specified period of the day, while the two older children were at school. Dawn, who was in kindergarten, came home at two o'clock and her time extended for the next half hour. Later in the afternoon, Willie, the eight-year-old, received his time.

Maline and Torrence's mother took a different approach. Instead of giving her children separate attention, she planned special activities that her children could do alongside each other. One day both children might put together puzzles, each doing his own puzzle on his own orange crate table. The next day they might do a coloring project or play with clay. This strategy required a lot of planning, but it worked well. Naturally, competition and rivalry still existed. Maline, who cer-

tainly sensed her coloring skills were not equal to those of her four-year-old brother, told us as she finished a drawing, "I go slow so I can make mine more prettier."

One of the most common methods for communicating equal consideration is to make sure that siblings take turns enjoying a special privilege. At Marguerita's house, for example, the children fought over saying the prayer before meals. The most sensible solution was to take turns, even though Marguerita's prayers did not make as much sense as her older brothers' prayers. Sometimes a simple chart helps keep track of whose turn it is. Frank, Constance, and Jeremy all wanted to go grocery shopping with their father, who was not home very much. Three at a time was too much, so a chart was set up to indicate whose turn it was to accompany Daddy to the store. A timer also may be appropriate for teaching children to take turns. Leontyne fought with her ten-year-old brother over who would get to sit in Daddy's chair to watch television. The problem was solved, or at least reduced in intensity, by setting a timer for ten minutes and letting the children switch seats at the sound of the bell.

It may seem contradictory to communicate equal love by reprimanding children, but some parents are often tempted to handle sibling rivalry that way. If sibling rivalry gets out of hand, and children resort to hurting each other, find a positive way to handle the situation. One technique is to remove the source of the controversy. This is a logical step but does not seem to be too successful with two-year-olds, who can easily find another reason to fight if so inclined. Many parents reported that the best solution was to separate the children. This punishment is also logical as it communicates to children that, if they cannot get along, they cannot play together. As Linn Su and Jenna's mother told us, "My girls can do without a specific toy, but it is harder to do without a companion. Within five minutes they have usually sneaked out of their rooms and are playing together quietly so I won't hear them."

It would be nice to be able to present families with the one best answer for "curing" sibling rivalry. However, as is always true in child rearing, there are no easy answers. Each family must work out a solution that is right for them. In the long run, the best way to reduce sibling rivalry is to encourage sibling cooperation. Torrence, who was four years old, had recently enlisted his two-year-old sister, Maline, as an ally. Together they explored the closets and hid behind the curtains. Torrence turned the lights off and then got under the sheet and made monster and ghost noises. "Scary, Mommy?" Maline would ask. Although their mother was not always enthusiastic about these joint endeavors, she tolerated them because they fostered a feeling of camaraderie between Maline and Torrence.

We observed a similar pattern between Kelly and her five-year-old brother, Kyle. They played happily in their room, making a huge pile of toys on the upper bunk bed. When it was time to wash up for lunch, they enjoyed splashing water on each other. At lunch, they sat at a little table in the kitchen while their mother cleaned the house. Instead of eating, they pushed the table back and forth, grabbed food from each other's plates and spilled their glasses of milk. The children may have been fighting, as their mother thought, but it seemed more likely to us that they had formed an alliance for the specific purpose of tormenting her.

Sibling cooperation, as well as sibling rivalry, can have its drawbacks. Still it is important to focus on the real advantages of being part of a family with more than one child. The child from a larger family has a twenty-four-hour on-call playmate. This playmate is a source of stimulation, companionship, and even protection. Many parents who complained about children fighting with each other on the homefront told us that, when other children were around, the older sibling watched over and protected the two-year-old. Being part of a larger family means increased social experience as well. Two-year-olds with older siblings learn how to initiate contact with other children, how to ignore minor hurts and falls, how to talk and joke with peers, and how to share the same toys. Having learned these social skills at home with brothers and sisters, it is easier to function in new situations with other children.

# MASTERY
# MOTIVATION

Danny's mother was expecting company. When she went into the living room to greet her guests, Danny slipped into the kitchen. A few seconds later Danny emerged holding a small lizard by the tail. "Look what I caught," Danny announced proudly.

Two-year-olds are full of energy, curiosity, and determination. From Danny's point of view he had made a great conquest, despite the horrified look of one of the guests. He was especially pleased with himself for catching the lizard by the tail, and could not understand why the guests didn't share his enthusiasm. The guests petted the dog when he went to the door, so how come they wouldn't pet the lizard?

In this section, we look at two kinds of achievements: learning language to communicate and mastering motor skills and play materials.

# CHAPTER 10

# *Developing Word Power*

W hile the motor skills of two-year-olds tend to develop at a steady rate, children's speaking skills often advance in sudden leaps. Due to these spurts in development, same-age peers may be in very different stages of language development.

*"I'm doing the farm puzzle," Jeannette announced as she struggled to fit a puzzle piece into the wrong place. "This is a hard piece. This is a very hard piece."*

*"Me do it," Suzanne insisted, taking the piece out of Jeannette's hand and putting it in the puzzle.*

*"This is my puzzle," Jeannette replied. "You can have the zoo puzzle. You like the zoo puzzle better?"*

*"Me, me, me do," Suzanne insisted again, and within a few minutes she had helped Jeannette complete the puzzle.*

Parents, overhearing this exchange between Jeannette and Suzanne, would be quick to note that Jeannette is by far the better talker. As Jeannette's parents, they might feel duly proud of their daughter's quickness. As Suzanne's parents, they might feel unnecessarily worried about their daughter's immature speech. However, it would be a mistake to conclude that Jeannette's precocious language development indicates greater intelligence. In fact, we do not know why some children, like Jeannette, are early talkers, but we do know that many of the differences between early and late talkers disappear by the time the children are three or four years old.

Whether a child is an early or late talker, significant growth takes place between two and three. Knowing more about the process of language development helps parents recognize and appreciate the progress their own child is making. In this chapter, we will discuss three aspects of language development. First, we will look at how two-year-old children expand their ability to listen to language and to understand what it means. Second, we will explore the process of learning to speak, combining sounds to make words and then combining words to make sentences. Finally, we will focus on how children learn to converse with other people, how they use both their listening and speaking skills to communicate. Throughout the chapter we also suggest ways to enrich the language environment of two-year-old children. These ideas are not intended to speed up language development but to make it more enjoyable for both parents and children.

# LEARNING TO LISTEN

When children appear to be slow in acquiring speech, but are on target in every other way, parents need to rule out a hearing problem. Between one and three years of age, some children develop temporary hearing problems from the build-up of fluid in their ears. The condition can be identified in a routine pediatric checkup and is usually controlled by medication. In a small number of cases, tubes are inserted into the child's ears to allow for appropriate drainage.

A second consideration with the slow-to-talk child is the development of listening skills. If a child who is not speaking listens to language being spoken and follows simple directions, parents have a right to relax. Comprehension precedes production and, before long, their child will be talking. When there is a significant language delay, the children do not comprehend the meaning of words.

## Listening Games

Parents who are concerned with encouraging language development can focus on listening games. One technique is to ask a series of "where" questions. Where questions, as opposed to what and why questions, can be answered nonverbally. For example, parents can pretend to lose or misplace something, and then invite their child to help with the search by asking questions out loud:

"Now, where are my sandals? Come here, sandals." (Turning to child.) "Do you have my sandals on? Hmmm, no you don't. Well, where are your sandals? Oh, you found them in the closet."

Probably the best version of this game occurs when parents look for missing children. Then they have the opportunity to stimulate listening by proposing the most absurd ideas. Stacey had recently learned to open closet doors, so whenever things got unusually quiet around the house her parents were pretty sure she was hiding in some closet. The only question was which one? "We better go find Stacey," her mother announced loudly in a typical incident. "Yes, let's try our bedroom first," answered Stacey's father in an equally loud voice. "Do you think she's in the jewelry box?" asked the mother. "Probably not," replied the father, "but she might be." "Hmm . . . not there," mused the mother. "Oh, no, I bet I threw her in the dirty clothes hamper by mistake this morning!" Long before her mother came up with this preposterous theory, Stacey's presence was made evident by her stifled giggles inside the closet. "Maybe I had better look in the closet before we go to the washing machine," Stacey's father suggested offhandedly. "Well, what do you know? Here she is, in our closet."

Singing to a two-year-old is another natural way to stimulate listening skills. Familiar songs can be elaborated by adding new verses. The general idea stays the same, which makes it easier for the child to understand, but each new verse creates a different image. "Old McDonald's Farm," for example, is a song of this type. Parents can keep thinking of new animals and new animal sounds for the farm. There is no reason, however, to stop with that. The farm can be populated with vehicles, machines, cow bells, squeaky doors, and anything else that makes a distinctive sound.

One day Shawn's father started to sing, "The Bear Went Over the Mountain," mainly because he couldn't think of any other song to sing. Shawn asked for more, so his father began to sing about transportation, a popular topic with Shawn. "The bear drove a motorcycle, the bear drove a motorcycle, the bear drove a motorcycle, up to the top of the mountain." "More," said Shawn. Soon the bear was driving all kinds of trucks and highway equipment. "Why just the bear?" thought Shawn's father, who was getting a little bored. "The lion drove the school bus . . . The mouse drove a fire engine . . . The giraffe came on roller skates." Shawn's father was enjoying the unique traffic jam on top of the mountain.

Listening games like the ones we have described are invariably products of the moment. Parents discover them as if by chance, because they take the time to relax and let their minds take off. Knowing what subjects are important to their child, they change the words of familiar songs to reflect their child's interest.

## *Listening to Books*

One of the most striking differences between the families we visited was their use of books. It was not uncommon for parents to tell us that they spent from two to four hours every day reading to their two-year-old. Other parents spent virtually no time reading to their children. However, even among families where it was obvious that books were seldom used, the children showed an intense interest when we began to read to them. The desire of a two-year-old to listen as an adult reads is an authentic phenomenon.

Two-year-olds who are learning to speak are especially interested in labeling pictures. They are attracted to books especially designed for this purpose; those by Richard Scary are

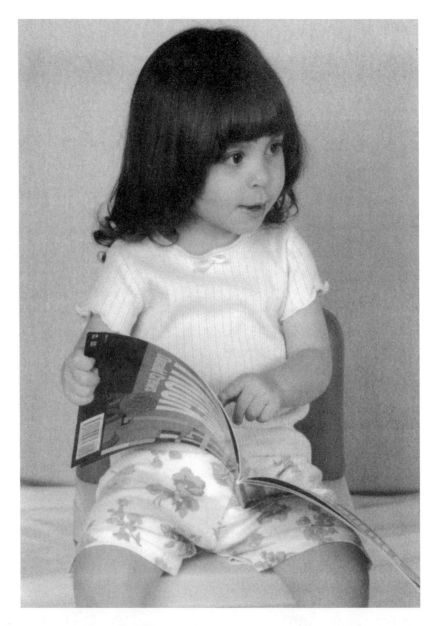

very popular. Children learn to recognize and to pronounce the names of exotic animals and specialized vehicles that they are not likely to see in the real world. In addition, there are numerous instances in which labeling within the simplified context of a book leads to recognition of real objects in the outside world.

Amy, for example, became interested in a book of signs. Her favorite sign was EXIT. To her parents' amazement, she began to point out EXIT signs in restaurants and stores. Then she started noticing STOP signs, IN and OUT signs, and ON signs. The sign book they read at home was clearly the inspiration for these discoveries.

The big leap in development occurs when children realize that there is a connection between the pages, and that the pictures and words tell a story. This discovery seems to be a gradual one, like piecing together a puzzle. Each time a favorite book is read, a bit more of the story is recognized. Erik's favorite book at two years of age was a book about a birthday

party. Having recently celebrated his own birthday, it was easier for him to follow the events in the story. Reading the book both refreshed his memory and gave him the opportunity to celebrate an imaginary party. If every day could not be his birthday, at least he could read the birthday book.

When children are first learning to follow a story, they insist on hearing it over and over. Parents get tired of this repetition but, in a surprisingly short time, two-year-olds become interested in a wide variety of story themes. Their powers of imagination develop to the point where they can enjoy stories about experiences they have never had, such as taking a trip in a rocket, digging for gold in the desert, or having a pet kangaroo.

Most children will have favorites, and whenever a story is connected to a special experience in their lives, that story may become a temporary obsession. Airplane trips may produce a burst of interest in airplane stories, feeding the animals on a farm can lead to a fascination with farm stories, a visit to the doctor often stimulates extra interest in stories about hospitals.

When parents get too bored by this constant repetition, they can try recording a story on tape. If two-year-old children are already familiar with a book, they are capable of listening to the taped story and turning the pages by themselves at the right moment.

Parents can also make reading more interesting for themselves by expanding a story. Although children do not like leaving out part of a story, they often welcome adding more to it. One way to embellish a story is to add dialogue. The pictures in most children's books include incidental characters, a squirrel in a tree, or a mouse behind a rock. These characters may not play a role in the story but there is no reason why they cannot become involved. If Curious George crashes his bike, the squirrel who is looking on in the picture can say, "I hope George is all right," or "I wish I had a bike like that," or any number of other things. Once children grasp the idea that any character in a story can talk at any time, they can create additional dialogue. When reading the story of the tortoise and the hare, for example, Nicole added that the hare was sleeping because he went to bed late last night (after visiting his cousins) and that he felt sad to sleep alone.

Two-year-old children are interested in stories that address their fears and anxieties. They are especially concerned about things being broken or lost, about people being injured or abandoned. It is no coincidence that the Curious George stories have been so popular for over thirty years. The two-year-old can easily identify with a little monkey who is always making a mess, breaking important objects, getting lost, or investigating forbidden places.

Sometimes children become so involved in the imaginative experience of a story that they cannot accept one of these fearful occurrences. Kori really liked stories about a giant dog named Clifford. Clifford had a habit of rolling over and smashing things that got in his way. In one story, he rolled on the family car and smashed it. Kori became quite upset and insisted, "Clifford did not smash car. Clifford did not smash car." The imaginative fear had become too real and Kori had to deny that it had happened. Kori's mother suggested that Clifford could fix the car. "No," replied Kori, "Clifford has no hands." Kori had become a strict realist as far as this event was concerned.

When children indicate an unwillingness to accept an imaginative experience that is too fearful, that part of the story can be skipped. Zachary, like many children, was straightforward in his solution to this problem. If he did not like part of a story, he announced, "The End," and slammed the book shut. Because young children cannot read by themselves, it is important to give them some degree of control over the activity. If they want to skip an objectionable page, or stop the story in the middle, parents should be accommodating.

## *Listening to Television*

Many two-year-olds like to watch "Sesame Street" or "Barney" and may have a few favorite cartoon shows, family shows, or other children's programs. Without a doubt they listen to the language on these programs, but our impression is that they concentrate on processing the visual in-formation. Television is primarily a visual medium, and the pace of information is fast and full of special effects. Two-year-old children certainly recognize familiar faces, like Bert and Ernie, from "Sesame Street." They may even recognize certain scripts associated with the Muppets or other favorite characters. But the meaning of Bert and Ernie's conversation does not seem to sink in very far. The children do not ask many questions about what they hear and they do not imitate the language of the Muppets in their own speech or imaginative play.

Most two-year-olds also are exposed to adult television programs. Invariably they pay more attention to the advertisements than to the programs. The nature of the product being advertised seems to be irrelevant. They are just as interested in a commercial for aspirin as they are in a toy advertisement. There are several reasons why a young child is so attracted to commercials. Commercials often include catchy music and an-imation. The close-ups of people staring straight into the cam-

era create a personal atmosphere that appeals to children. Yet the impression remains that two-year-olds are drawn to commercials because of the language. They seem to be listening to the words, even though many of them are too hard to understand. Whenever the commercial is shown, the same words are heard, each one following the other in a completely predictable pattern. For this reason, commercials represent a chance for two-year-olds to practice their listening skills. It is a challenge to anticipate and then confirm the sequence of words.

When children indicate that they are learning to recognize television commercials, it is a sign that they are ready to listen to simple story tapes. Tapes consisting of stories no longer than a few minutes are available. These tapes have the same appeal as commercials: clearly articulated language, a musical background, and a short message that can be repeated over and over. The listening stimulation they provide, however, is much more meaningful to two-year-olds than that of television commercials.

Whether children are listening to a story tape or an appropriate television program, this kind of listening activity is less flexible and less personal than other activities we have discussed. Singing a song, reading a book, or playing a listening game involves personal interaction between parents and children. These activities are adapted to fit individual interests and styles. They are open-ended rather than fixed, alive rather than canned. The performance on a television program may be much more polished and entertaining, but two-year-olds generally prefer to listen to a real person who knows them. Sitting on a lap and reading a book is better than watching the best that show business can offer.

Of course, real people are not always available to talk to a two-year-old and, in these situations, it is reasonable to substitute electronically produced language. But even when children are encouraged to sit in front of a television set or tape machine, the experience will be more productive if parents participate to some degree. Parents can talk occasionally with the children about what is happening. They can note the topics that most intrigue their children and bring them up in future conversations. Television and other electronic media represent an ever-present source of stimulation and, when used sparingly, add variety and spice to the language environment of two-year-olds. However, when used so often that they replace listening activities with real people, these technological marvels actually impoverish the language environment of young children.

# EXPRESSIVE LANGUAGE

Learning to listen may be basic to language development, but learning to speak is more significant to parents. We eagerly anticipate a child's first words, and when they appear we start listening for the child's first sentences. There often is a relatively long time—six months or more—during which a child's speaking ability seems to expand slowly. This dormant period typically occurs between one and two years of age. When it happens, parents become worried: "Coretta understands almost everything we say, and she can pronounce words. Why doesn't she talk more?" Then one day Coretta's parents realize that her vocabulary is bursting with new words. Now she only needs to hear a word once before it is picked up.

This pattern of slow, almost nonexistent vocabulary growth, followed by a rapid spurt, is quite common. One reason seems to be that, during the period of slow growth, children are learning how to control different speech sounds. Once they have mastered enough sounds to repeat many of the words they hear, their speaking vocabulary suddenly expands.

We take for granted this ability to imitate speech, but in reality it is a small miracle. Without observing the tongue and palate movements that are necessary to produce each consonant and vowel, children somehow learn to make these sounds and to coordinate them into words. A word like "helicopter," for example, requires a complicated sequence of speech acts. No wonder a child just starting to speak may say "heh" or "caw" or mumble something unintelligible. If a two-year-old child's understanding of language is progressing satisfactorily and yet the child is slow to speak, he may be having a problem with articulation. Usually children solve these articulation problems by themselves in a few months and rapidly catch up in speaking skills.

The best way to encourage two-year-olds to improve their articulation is to give them opportunities to talk to a wide range of people. Gillian used to talk on the telephone to her father at the office every day. Other people in the office also wanted to say hello. Gillian usually called right after lunch and she often reported on the food she did not like. "I no like cely" she an-

nounced one day. "You don't like jelly?" the secretary asked. "No, no," said Gillian. "I no like cely." "I don't understand you, Gillian," answered the secretary "Soup," Gillian explained. Although the secretary never did figure out that Gillian meant celery soup, our example illustrates the process by which misunderstanding creates pressure for better articulation.

## *The Transition From Inflection to Words*

Talking is a matter of inflection as well as words. Inflection is the music of speech: the pitch and tone of voice and the rhythm of phrases. Babies are more attentive to inflection than to words. When spoken in a horrified tone of voice, a word like "hot" communicates a sense of danger to babies long before they understand the specific meaning of the word. Between the ages of one and two, many children demonstrate an amazing control of inflection. They chatter away in familiar inflection patterns, and their language sounds real to us even though we cannot identify the words.

Toddlers use their control of inflection to communicate. They send inflectional messages that mean "I'm happy, I'm angry, I want more food, I want out of my crib, I want to be carried." Using words to communicate feelings or wants represents a new strategy, and some children seem unwilling to give up the old style that parents already understand.

At eighteen months, Angeline had mastered every detail of the daily schedule and was clever at getting what she wanted. If she wanted to hear a story, she would hand a book to her mother, make an excited, pleading sound, and then clap her hands. Angeline's mother knew the routine was manipulative but it was so cute. Angeline's father, on the other hand, responded well when Angeline stamped her little foot and made a menacing sound with her voice. He found this "fierce" behavior quite charming. Not surprisingly, Angeline was not talking at twenty-four months. Her parents recognized the importance of not responding too quickly to Angeline's nonverbal language, and before long Angeline communicated with words. Because her parents had been responsive to her communications, it was not difficult for Angeline to change her primary language from inflection to verbalization.

Although Angeline's family encouraged her to talk in words, their responsiveness to her nonverbal communication built a foundation for later language development. Jennifer's mother demonstrated another technique for laying the foundation for language development. At one-year-old, Jennifer had developed a pointing game. As soon as her mother picked her up, she pointed to a window or picture across the room. She expected her mother to go over there and talk about what she was seeing.

*Mother: "Look, Jennifer, there's a bird out in the tree. Isn't she a pretty bird?"*
*Jennifer: "Da, da."*
*Mother: "That's right, there is some dirt on the window."*
*Jennifer: "Da, da."*
*Mother: "Oh, you want down? O. K."*

*Jennifer: "Da, da."*
*Mother: "Oh, I see what you got, your duck."*
*Jennifer: "Da, da."*
*Mother: "Yes, the duck is like the bird in the tree. Very good."*

Jennifer's mother discovered a multitude of messages in Jennifer's "Da, da." Perhaps some of these messages were not even there; it does not really matter. The important thing is her mother's orientation. She assumes that the more she responds to Jennifer's messages, no matter how ill-formed, the more messages Jennifer will send. In our experience, this is exactly what happens. Jennifer's mother usually responds with some verbalization. Even when she is granting a request, such as putting Jennifer down, she describes the action. By modeling a variety of messages, she undoubtedly helps Jennifer to formulate her own.

Jennifer is still using inflections and gestures as her primary means of communication. At some point she will need to abandon this strategy in favor of words. In Jennifer's case, we can predict this transfer will be accomplished easily; so easily, in fact, that her parents may never notice it. Jennifer will find the transition simple because she has so many different messages to send. She will not be satisfied much longer to point in the general direction she wants her mother to go. She will start pointing at specific objects, wanting to hold them and wanting her mother to talk about them. Pointing to the cupboard when she is hungry will be even less satisfactory. She may get a cracker when she wants the honey. As the specificity of her messages increases, so will her incentive to use words.

We do not want to imply that when children are slow to talk it necessarily means their parents are unresponsive. There are a number of possible reasons for delayed speech. Our point is that trying to force children to talk is not a particularly effective way to develop language. We recommend trying to expand the number of messages children want to send. Parents can encourage more messages by pointing out interesting sights, by describing their children's actions, by playing listening games, and by reading books. We believe that if children want to communicate a variety of messages, they will eventually find the words.

## Combining Words into Sentences

Once children begin to use a large variety of one-word messages, it is only a matter of a few weeks or months before the words are combined into sentences. Some children go through a stage of two-word sentences, followed by three- and then four-word sentences, systematically building their grammatical expertise. Other children use familiar phrases and simple sentence frames from the start. The progression from one to several words is impressive enough, but the grammatical elaboration that soon follows is truly astounding. After six months to a year of talking in sentences, children acquire the basic grammar of their native language.

Grammar learning is accomplished without any direct instruction from adults. Children listen to the language around them and come up with their own rules of grammar. Imitation plays a part in that children pick up the phrases and vocabulary of their parents, but all children have their own systems for creating sentences.

We know young children have their own rules of grammar because they systematically make mistakes they have never heard. For example, a two-year-old may say, "Me going store." The child has never heard anyone else use "me" like this. However, he has learned from listening that "me" is used as a self-referent, and therefore he uses it in all cases. We might say that he has learned part of a standard English rule.

The grammar of children is sometimes more logical than the grammar of their parents. Children learn and use the rule before they learn the exceptions. For example, when children learn to form plurals by adding an "s," they change foot to foots or feets. When they learn to form the past tense by adding "ed," they change go to goed and hit to hitted.

Between the ages of two and three, children learn to fill in the little words that are missing in their earlier sentences. "Me going Mama store," becomes "I am going with my Mama to the store." Words like "the," "with," "my," and "to" are not usually necessary to understand simple sentences, but they specify the meaning more precisely. One day parents suddenly realize that their children are routinely inserting common prepositions and adjectives into sentences.

There are two kinds of sentences that are particularly difficult to construct, although both are common. These sentences are questions and negative statements. Their combination, a negative question, is even harder. Parents can watch their two-year-olds progressing step by step with these sentences. One of the first steps in forming questions is to learn special question words that can be placed at the beginning of a sentence: "Why you fixing my tricycle?" "Where we going?" A second step, which often does not begin to appear until the age of three, is to use the correct helping verb at the beginning of the question: "Why are you fixing my tricycle?" "Where are we going?" The development of negative sentences is somewhat similar. At first children learn to add a negative word to the sentence: "I no like dogs." "I not going home." Later they begin to add the appropriate helping verb: "I am not going home." "I do not like dogs."

We have greatly simplified the complexities of questions and negative sentences. Most two-year-olds have only begun the process of learning these rules. Several more years of listening and talking will be needed before children fully understand them. The best way to help children develop grammatical competence is to expose them to many examples of proper grammar and to encourage them to express themselves as much as possible. As we emphasized with articulation, it is conversation and not instruction that is the key to language development.

Two-year-old children also practice their grammar by talking to themselves. Typically, these monologues occur when children are quietly occupied—going to sleep, playing in the bathtub, or riding in a car. A child may start with a simple phrase and build it up into a more complex one: "Bye bye, Nana. Have a nice time working on papers, Nana." The reverse exercise may occur, breaking a long phrase down into a simple one. "Ring around, falling down." Sometimes children invent substitute words: "Riding on a camel, riding on a boat, riding on a plane," or they practice making negative statements, "The car's too hot. Not too hot; it's too far. Not too far." Other drills may involve pronouns, pluralization, or any other grammatical rules children incorporate into their language at this age. The desire of children to master the rules of grammar is an amazing phenomenon.

# CONVERSATIONS

*Willie:* "I want ketchup."
*Mother:* "Don't you remember, you broke it yesterday?"
*Willie:* "We buy more ketchup at store?"
*Mother:* "Sure, next time we go. How about mustard for your sandwich?"
*Willie:* "This mustard bites my mouth."
*Mother:* "Here, let's mix it with some mayonnaise."
*Willie:* "I don't like mayonnaise."
*Mother:* "Sure you do. You always eat it with salami."
*Willie:* "This is not salami. It's olive loaf."
*Mother:* "Well, it's the same thing really. Anyway, this isn't mayonnaise. It's mustardaise."
*Willie:* "Yea, mustardaise, we don't have no ketchupaise. Just mustardaise."
*Mother:* "And it will make your ears grow."

A conversation is both an exchange of information and a social interaction. Within the back and forth rhythm, we can see that Willie has developed considerable conversational skill. He can form questions, arguments, comments, and even a joke. As in many conversations with two-year-olds, Willie's primary purpose in this exchange is to get adult help. He wants some improvement in his sandwich, and he uses language to affect his mother's behavior. Although the conversation does not focus on new information, several ideas are communicated. Ketchup comes from stores, mayonnaise cuts the strong taste of mustard, and olive loaf is like salami. There also is a playful aspect to this conversation. Both the mother and Willie are having fun playing with their ideas and their word games as though they are both children discovering new ways to use words. Willie argues only half-heartedly about the mayonnaise and, when his mother invents a new term, he plays with it and comes up with his own new word. Using language to affect another person's behavior, to communicate ideas, and just for fun are the three aspects of conversation we will discuss in more detail.

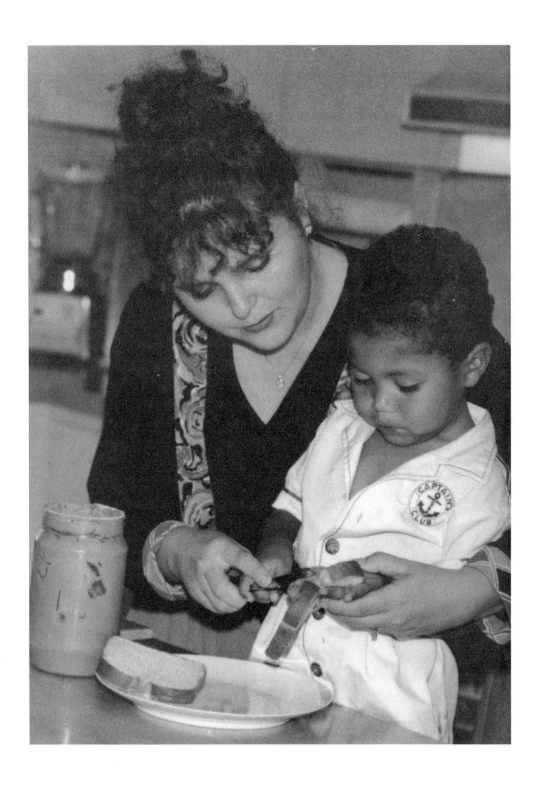

## *Affecting Another Person's Behavior*

At an early age, children begin to use language to make their wishes known. Between the ages of two and three, they learn to back up these requests with arguments. The "no" of the toddler gives way to more sophisticated forms of self-assertion. As Kori put it when she was told to go inside, "I am Myla Kori Bardige, and I'm not going inside." Loosely translated, this argument seems to be, "I am an important person and, therefore, when I say no, it carries weight."

There is a strong imitative element in these early arguments. Kori's mother used Kori's full name when she meant business, and Kori was imitating this practice. Such imitative language is usually easy to tolerate because it is so entertaining. Brandon told his mother, "You drive me up a wall," when he was told to take a nap, and Erik snorted, "fridiculous," when told to put on his coat before going outside.

Two-year-olds go beyond using imitative language to contradict their parents. They also turn parents' arguments back on them. Lisa liked to answer the phone, and she resisted giving the phone to her mother by saying, "You don't know them." Randy refused to eat his dinner because, "I'm a baby and babies don't have to eat dinner." Matthew told his father, "You have to share your tools with me cause I share my tools with you."

When children use the phrases and arguments of their parents, they probably do not control their parents' behavior, but at least some of the tension is released. Sometimes parents laugh and agree with the child's point of view; sometimes they insist on their own perspective, but in a gentler tone of voice. Although the arguments of two-year-old children often make us smile, we should remember that they are serious. Children do not argue with us in order to be amusing, but in order to make a point. Sooner or later they will push their arguments far enough to annoy us or even to make us angry, and to announce that they are older and bigger and that's why we need to listen to them.

It was funny the first time Patty said she was "too busy" to put on her clothes. After being late to nursery school every day for two weeks, however, the situation was different. Stacey's mother smiled when Stacey said she was "not perky" and needed another vitamin pill. But Stacey could not be convinced that one was enough, and she turned breakfast into a tense time by continually whining, "I need more."

Probably the most difficult kind of argument to handle is being told to be quiet. Kyle told his parents to stop reminding him about the toilet by saying, "I want done that." Other children are even more direct. They cut parents off in the middle of their lectures by saying, "No talk" or "Go away." These responses are infuriating to parents who are already inflamed.

On the one hand, it is unrealistic to anticipate laughing off every argument that a two-year-old formulates. On the other hand, it does not make much sense to go to the other extreme and punish a two-year-old for arguing or talking back. The most primitive and least flexible way to exercise control in a conversation is to force the conversation to end, and this is what we do when we do not allow children to argue with us. The ability of two-year-old children to argue follows naturally from their growing conversational skill. If we refuse to let children argue with us, we are encouraging them to drop out of future conversations by ignoring us. They may appear to be more polite, but what they are really doing is paying less attention to us.

Many arguments with two-year-old children cannot be resolved satisfactorily because the children do not understand the concepts involved in the argument. For example, when Timothy's parents told him that he needed to go to bed in order to rest, he insisted that he was not tired. Indeed, his en-

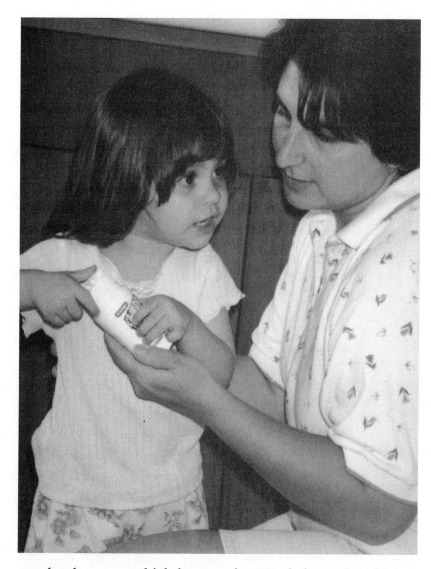

ergy level was very high because he speeded up when he got tired. Telling Timothy that he needed rest because he would be very busy after his nap was no good either. He could not understand the relationship between rest and energy, and his ability to project himself into the future was quite imprecise.

Timothy's parents realized that he did not understand their explanations, but they still allowed Timothy to argue with them. They accepted Timothy's feelings that this issue was an important topic for conversation.

The more young children argue, the better they become at it and the more likely they are to gain a compromise. At some point every parent reaches a limit and refuses to argue about a subject any more. But until that point is reached, two-year-old children are learning about a valuable aspect of conversation, the fine art of negotiation and compromise.

When compromise is not possible, children may opt for saving face. One day Stacey did not like what the family was having for dinner. "I want a hot dog," she told her mother. "I'm sorry, we don't have any," was the reply. Stacey consoled herself by saying "Maybe tomorrow." Her mother doubted that hot dogs would be served the next day, but she let the comment pass, knowing that by tomorrow Stacey would have forgotten about it. Beverly's attempt to save face was even more transparent. She was denied dessert because she had not eaten her dinner, and as the rest of the family ate their ice cream she rationalized, "I don't like ice cream anyway." Having the last word is a Pyrrhic victory, but it often is sufficient for two-year-old children. Not able to control the situation, they can at least control the conversation.

In many conversations that focus on the communication of ideas, two-year-old children take the role of asking questions. Although questions may be used to tease parents or simply to extend a conversation, two-year-olds also use questions to solicit information. "What's that?" may be a genuine question when a child sees an unusual object and wants to know its name. Another early question is "where?" and some very interesting "where" questions may appear as children become more aware of disappearing objects. Mason asked where a balloon was after it had popped. Constance asked where Big Bird went after the television had lost its picture. Matthew asked where the soapsuds went as they dribbled down the drain.

"Why" questions are a new development between two and three. It often takes a while for children to grasp the meaning of "why." Once they learn to use this question form appropriately, they tend to ask about the purpose or intention behind events. "Why you spank the cat?" "Why you painting house?"

Accidents are particularly hard to explain. Kelly asked her mother several times a day for a week, "Why Daddy drop peanut butter?" With less patience each time, her mother explained that it had been an accident, the peanut butter had slipped, Daddy wasn't using both hands. Kelly found these explanations unsatisfactory because they did not specify an intention or a purpose. Breaking the peanut butter jar was not an intentional act and neither did it serve any purpose. So Kelly remained confused as to why it had happened, and she kept asking for clarification.

Another new question form between the ages of two and three is "Who?" Children discover that every person has a name. Naturally they expect their parents to know these names, just as they know the names of objects. A child may ask for the name of the mailman or the trash collector, the clerks in the stores, other passengers in an elevator, or even for the names of people driving by in cars.

The ability of young children to express sequential information is limited, but they do show a great desire to talk about the past. Parents find themselves describing the events of the day to their two-year-olds as they go to sleep at night. This routine starts innocently enough, for it is natural to remind children of a pleasant experience before they drift off to sleep. However, the intense interest of many children in these reminiscences leads to more and more detailed conversation.

Extended conversation about any topic leads away from the immediate time and place. Having just begun to communicate in sentences, two-year-olds are eager to explore this transcendent quality of language. Their capacity to appreciate remote times and places may be somewhat limited. The place they describe may be the neighborhood drug store and the time may be earlier that day. Their memory may seem rigid, almost mechanical, to us. Every time Halloween was mentioned, Jeffrey said, "Remember the spider?" referring to an impressive Halloween display he had seen at the grocery store. Yet he continued to listen intently to his mother's recollections of putting on his costume, giving out candy, and trick or treating.

## Conversational Play and Humor

One of the functions of language at every age is play. The toddler who babbles happily as he removes books from the bookcase is bubbling over with good cheer. He is not trying to control or communicate, just to celebrate his mood with some verbal music. More and more of this music is set to words as the language of children matures. The two-year-old who is dunking her doll in the bathtub repeats to herself in a sing-song chant, "In and out. In and out." Almost every monologue has elements of playful poetry, even if its primary purpose is to guide or clarify the child's activity. As Linn Su drew a picture, she murmured, "Where did my chalk go? I am making a nice circle here. Where's the sponge, hon? Here's the sponge, hon."

The appearance of verbal humor is another new development between the ages of two and three. As children come to understand the sense of language, they see the humor of nonsense. Nouns predominate in the early language of children and therefore noun nonsense predominates in early humor.

Peter did a double-take the first time his mother asked him if he wanted some more "blibber." She had a dish of noodles in her hand. "Was this some kind of trick?" he wondered. "Do you want some more blibber? Or is it blubber?" "No," roared Peter, "just noodles," and he grabbed the dish. The

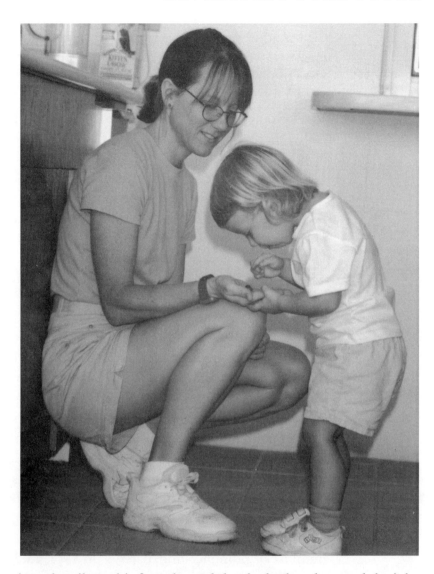

broad smile on his face showed that he had understood the joke and was waiting for more of this crazy talk.

Noun nonsense evolves naturally from nursery rhymes that children have memorized. "Mary had a little elephant," recited Brenan's mother, as Brenan giggled. Zachary, who didn't like sad endings anyway, was much happier when the last little piggy went to the Pizza Hut instead of home.

Another natural opportunity to introduce humor arises when two-year-old children start the game of "what's this?" After dinner every night Brandon insisted that his father sit down and look at a Richard Scary book with him. "What's this?" Brandon asked, pointing to a picture of a fried egg. "Why, that's a fried floozle," said his father. "No, silly, that's an egg."

Of course, the unparalleled master of noun nonsense is Dr. Seuss. Most of his stories are too complicated for two-year-old children to follow, but they enjoy listening to the word concoctions. A particular phrase may get singled out and become part of a daily game. For example, Andy liked the phrase "a wocket in your pocket," so his parents amused him with similar questions, "Is there a wup in your cup? Is there a wub in the tub?"

Two-year-old children are also beginning to enjoy the humor of mispronunciation. Brenan quickly picked up his parents' nighttime routine of asking, "Are you thoisty?" In Stacey's family, everyone gets a "hugarooni," which sounds a lot more special than the normal hug. Families make up strange and humorous pet names for each other, such as "Weenie Brandini," or "Jody Pody" and "Sherry Cherrie."

Language teaching is a role that most parents both assume and enjoy. The speed at which two-year-olds learn vocabulary, pronunciation, grammar, and conversational skills is astounding. Although some parents are tempted to correct their child's grammar or pronunciation, parents do a splendid job of stimulating their two-year-old's language. They respond to their children's queries, answering both questions and complaints. They read many books with their children in a way that is both informative and entertaining. Most importantly, they engage their child in a back and forth conversation. As parents talk with their child, sharing feelings and ideas, they experience a new kind of closeness and a new sense of intimacy.

# CHAPTER 11

# *Having Fun*

~~~~~~~~~~~~~~~~~~~~~~~~~~~~~~~~~

*Jermaine was in the sandbox, dumping sand out of his dump truck and filling it back up again.*

*Mother: "Jermaine, I've told you three times already. We have to go in and have lunch."*

*Jermaine: "Can't go. I too busy working."*

From a child's point of view, there is no distinction between work and play. Whether they are filling a dump truck, scribbling on a wall with crayons, or jumping over cracks in the sidewalk, whether you call it work or play, they have an important job. In this chapter, we look at two types of play: Active Play and Constructive Play.

## ACTIVE PLAY

Allison was sitting at her chair in the dining room, tilting her chair back and forth. Her parents were attempting to talk with each other, and her tilting game was annoying. "Please be still," her father pleaded. "I am trying to talk with your mother." "I am being still," Allison countered. "I am sitting down in the chair."

Two-year-olds have trouble staying still. Even when they are exploring a puzzle, a set of blocks or a toy workbench, they are up and down, circling around, squatting, standing, running to the window. Moving around is an important part of explo-

ration. The children are discovering the possibilities and limitations of their own bodies, and at the same time they are learning about the space that surrounds them.

Toddlers are interested in testing themselves against large and cumbersome objects. They strain to push, pull, and lift these obstacles. Two-year-olds continue this kind of body exploration, although their interest seems to be waning. The primary mode of the active two-year-old is no longer pushing or carrying, but running. Children at this age are inveterate runners. They are willing to run even when they are too tired to walk. However, the racing technique of older children has not yet been mastered. Two-year-olds may run with gusto, but their short, choppy steps go nowhere fast. And trying to turn a sharp corner often results in an abrupt and painful landing.

Running and jumping go together. Between two and three years of age, children learn to put a little hop, skip, or jump into their running. When we say "little," we do not exaggerate. Running and jumping over a sock or a hose is considered quite an accomplishment.

Jumping with the aid of a spring is a different matter. Heather demonstrated for us the typical exuberance with which a two-year-old rides a rocking horse. The higher the bounce, the better the ride. Similar creatures are available in

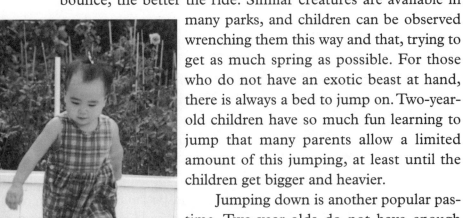

many parks, and children can be observed wrenching them this way and that, trying to get as much spring as possible. For those who do not have an exotic beast at hand, there is always a bed to jump on. Two-year-old children have so much fun learning to jump that many parents allow a limited amount of this jumping, at least until the children get bigger and heavier.

Jumping down is another popular pastime. Two-year-olds do not have enough strength to jump up very far, but they do have the nerve to jump down, especially if a soft landing is provided for them. We watched Christopher and Peter jumping off a coffee table onto a cushion on the floor. The first jump was approached with trepidation, but after that they jumped with the abandon of experienced paratroopers.

Most two-year-olds continue to develop their climbing skills, but there are large differences between individual children. Some children are fearful of heights, while others demonstrate a new strength and agility in their climbing. Brandon showed us how he climbed up on the bar to watch the fish. Matthew was one of several children who enjoyed climbing in and out of a crib.

Climbing outside was more difficult. The bars on jungle gyms seem too far apart for most two-year-olds and the drop to the bottom too great a fall. Jason, who was a talented climber, was willing to try a jungle gym only when his mother was nearby to catch him. Climbing a tree presented similar difficulties. Matthew enjoyed the view but required assistance getting up and down. Climbing a ladder on a slide, or scaling a chain link fence, were more satisfactory challenges for the two-year-olds we visited.

Throwing is a body movement that often develops dramatically between two and three. Toddlers flip objects more than they throw them. They do not get their bodies behind the throw, and they have only a slight ability to aim. The object may be released too early and fall behind the child. If not, it is likely to go flying off at almost any angle. By the age of three, however, children can aim their throws, although they may choose to tease an adult by throwing a ball in the wrong direction. Because of their greater ability to throw, two-year-olds like to play with small balls that can be grasped in one hand. This is in contrast to the preference of toddlers for large balls that can be lugged around.

Small balls are for throwing, large ones are for catching. Willie was able to catch a volleyball by trapping it against his body. This ability was decidedly limited, though. The ball had to be thrown from a very short distance and it had to hit Willie

squarely in the chest. Suzanne, on the other hand, was able to catch a large balloon with just her hands. The balloon traveled through the air so slowly that she could track its motion and respond accordingly.

Body movements of all kinds are involved in gymnastics. Two-year-olds are awed by the gymnastic skills of a five-year-old, but their ability to join in is rather limited. Somersaults are practiced diligently, and, if someone is available to assist, two-year-olds like to stand on their heads. Dancing represents a kind of gymnastics that is more manageable. We watched Angeline dance enthusiastically to a Barney tape. Her dancing was full of vigorous arm and leg movements, quite a change from the restrained bounce of a toddler.

The arm and leg coordination that enables two-year-olds to run and jump and dance can be applied to a tricycle. Wheels can replace feet as a means of transportation. This is not an instantaneous process, however. Children do not realize the initial force that is necessary to overcome inertia, and they are not sure when each foot should be pressed down on the pedal. The first movements are a matter of inches and, as Jason demonstrated for us, they are just as likely to be in a backward

as a forward direction. The best practicing surface is one that slopes very slightly downhill. Too steep a hill may lead to catastrophe, while the smallest upgrade will stop a novice cyclist in his tracks. The two-year-old who gets too frustrated by the whole process will get off and push. In fact, some children get so good at pushing and steering simultaneously that they do not even attempt to ride. Then one day they begin to pedal and, in a short time, they are riding as if they had been doing it all their lives.

A similar kind of coordination is involved in pumping a swing, but most children take longer to learn that. Perhaps it is because parents are more willing to push a swing than a tricycle. Wherever two-year-olds gather, sooner or later, they will be found sitting in swings, being pushed by older persons. For the two-year-old, swinging is a relaxing activity that children and parents share: a time for talking and laughing together. At some point in the future, parents will expect their children to do the work themselves but, for the time being, they are happy to play a helping role.

In general, playgrounds are a happy place for two-year-olds and their parents. Most of the children have overcome earlier fears of slides or swings. Yet they are not quite ready to join in the rough and tumble play of older children. Parents do not have to stand over the children in fear that they are going to get hurt, but at the same time they are still needed: to push the merry-go-round gently, to catch children at the bottom of a tall slide, to help children get down from a platform. It is a situation in which parents can both relax and participate.

There are other ways in which parents and two-year-olds share physical activity. Kyle initiated wrestling matches by jumping on his father whenever he lay down. When Shawn's mother propped her legs on the coffee table, Shawn used them like a bar for somersaulting to the floor. Jeannette and her mother liked to put on a tape and intersperse their housework with dancing. This is the most interesting characteristic of physical exploration—it invariably leads to a shared activity.

These shared activities have the qualities of a game. There are no winners or losers, but there are unwritten rules that parents and children follow. Running leads to chase games, chasing evolves into a simple version of hide and seek. The children run away and hide, knowing full well that their parents will find them because they always hide in the same place. This spot is likely to be a small space, such as a box, a clothes basket, or a space behind the sofa into which the child can just barely squeeze. Chase games may be elaborated verbally with two-year-olds. For example, Jason's father sang, "All Around the Mulberry Bush" as he chased Jason. The words were adapted to fit the situation: "All around the living room, Daddy chased Jason; Jason sat down in a chair, and Daddy sat down on him."

Jumping leads to jumping games. Usually the child is the jumper, and the parent is the catcher. Whenever Zachary saw his father was close enough, he jumped off the kitchen chair or off the crib railing. There wasn't much his father could do but catch Zachary; and so far, his father told us, he has not missed. We suspect he enjoyed catching Zachary. Erik requested a jumping game while shopping. Each parent held one of his hands while saying, "Jack be nimble, Jack be quick, Jack jump over the candlestick." On the word "over," Erik jumped as high as he could. At the same time his parents lifted him, and he seemed to jump two or three feet in the air.

Throwing leads to games of catch. Zachary demonstrated a version of the game favored by two-year-olds. Before going to sleep, he threw all his stuffed animals out of the crib while his father tried to catch them. Jason and his mother used a bathtub for their game of catch. While Jason was in the tub, his mother tossed him a ball. Inevitably, Jason missed the ball, but it floated right next to him and was easy to retrieve. Jason flung the wet ball back to his mother, who threw him a high one that made a big splash as it landed.

Running, jumping, and throwing are the activities that seem to stimulate the greatest number of parent-child play routines. However, we observed other examples. In Matthew's home, father-son wrestling led to a pretend boxing game. Riding a tricycle became a game for Linn Su when she rode through a tunnel formed by her father's legs. Zachary and his parents played a dancing game called "circle" when they played Zachary's favorite tape. Every form of physical activity has the potential of becoming a shared game.

One reason games occur in connection with physical activity is that both children and parents think it is important to develop physical skills. Parents enjoy teaching children how to use their bodies, and they take a great deal of pride in the growing physical ability of their children. This feeling of pride is reflected by the children. Brandon showed us how he could do a somersault. Jodi was proud of being able to stand up in a swing. Daniel jumped into the pool and swam back to the side. "See, Mommy," he announced proudly, "I made it."

# CONSTRUCTIVE PLAY

Jody was sitting in her booster chair at the kitchen table. She shaped her potatoes into a mound, and pushed her bread sticks inside. "You know you are not supposed to play with food," her

mother scolded. "Food is to eat, and toys are to play with."

"I'm not playing," Jody insisted. "I am building a castle."

At two years old, children are just grasping the idea that one thing can stand for another. A pile of mashed potatoes can represent a sand castle. Yellow circles crayoned on the wall paper can represent a sun. A wiggly line of blocks can represent a bumpy road. Two-year-olds seldom demonstrate artistic talents, but they have grasped the notion that they can make up or rearrange stuff and it can turn out to be something different, and something to be proud of.

## *Arts, Crafts, and Sculpture*

Two-year-olds enjoy creating with glue, paper, and clay. But unless they are helped by a parent, their creations are likely to look more like a mess than an artistic creation. Most of all, children enjoy manipulating materials: pounding and rolling the clay, tearing the paper, and spreading the paste on everything in their reach. But despite their random manipulations, they do mean to create something. "See, Mommy," Alesha announced proudly as she handed her mother a sticky paper plate covered with torn paper.

Two-year-olds, unless their parent takes the lead, cannot create a craft or a sculpture. However, they do enjoy the process and, like Alesha, are proud of the end product. Kori succeeded in using up half a roll of scotch tape sticking it on the dining room table. Jeannette tore up a letter, dropped the pieces on the table, and announced that it was raining. Jeremy got hold of a piece of play dough and flattened it on his dinner dish. These children were not attempting to get into mischief. They were, as a matter of fact, quite pleased with their creations.

## *Drawing*

When we arrived at Kyle's house, his mother told us that Kyle really "had a thing" about smiley faces. He practiced drawing them on every possible occasion. A little while later we went outside, and Kyle quite spontaneously confirmed his mother's statement. He picked up a chunk of limestone from the driveway and used it to draw a perfectly recognizable smiley face in the middle of the sidewalk. As Kyle sat back to admire his product, it was obvious that he was not just exploring the properties of the limestone. He was interested in the fact that he had created a face.

Occasionally, a two-year-old begins with the notion of drawing a particular object, as with Kyle and his smiley faces. More frequently, he begins by making the drawing and the identification comes afterwards. After scribbling with a blue crayon, Jodi looked at her drawing and said, "Look at the blue doggy Jodi made." Often the same object reappears in different scribbles. Nicole saw elephants and triangles; Jermaine saw suns and moons; Matthew saw bananas and apples. Adults encourage the tendency to see things in a scribble, but it is such a persistent phenomenon that it seems to spring primarily from the perception of the child. Many times, but not always, there really is a form in the scribble that suggests the object the child names.

The drawing of most two-year-olds may lack planning, but it does not lack structure. There are discernible elements in this scribbling. One child may make circular scribbles while another makes jagged up and down lines that look something like a picket fence. In addition, two-year-olds often distinguish between drawing and writing elements. Matthew, for example, drew either big circles or teeny closed shapes. Lisa created circles or half-inch-long lines. Shawn made either line scribbles or little chicken scratches. These children reported objects in their larger drawings, but words in their little scribbles.

Usually two-year-olds use a small number of colors in each drawing. Their use of color seems to change as they become more familiar with a particular medium. Children who are just starting to use crayons tend to complete a scribble with one crayon, while those with several months' experience begin to combine colors. When watercolors or tempera are first used, the children may go through a period in which they create a blob of a single color. Later on, a variety of shapes and colors is more likely. The preferred medium for many children is the felt-tip pen. Felt tips combine a fine point for easy scribbling with the vivid color of paints.

It is quite a revelation to young children that representational objects can be drawn. In our culture children are surrounded by pictures, and they learn to recognize pictures at an early age. It is usually considerably later, however, that they realize pictures can be drawn. Many of the two-year-olds in our study were so captivated by this discovery that they asked their parents to draw for them.

Although parents often express embarrassment over their own artistic skills, two-year-olds are not a critical audience. Once parents take the plunge and start to draw, both parents and children enjoy themselves. A parent whose drawing is a bit rusty can begin with simple objects, such as chocolate chip cookies or ice cream cones, and then work up to fire engines and bears. The objective is not to teach young children to draw, but to respond to their interests, to follow a line of exploration they cannot pursue by themselves.

Some two-year-olds like to scribble over drawings. For example, after asking his mother to draw garbage trucks, Andy would color all over the picture. He did not seem to be trying to destroy the drawing so much as to participate in its creation. Frequently two-year-olds respond in this way to coloring books. They scribble over the pictures without the slightest concern about using "proper" colors. The printed pictures inspire the children to experiment with their own artistic skills.

Some people worry that exposing children to adult drawing, or giving them coloring books, will stunt their artistic development. Our experience indicates just the opposite. Two-year-old children welcome outside stimulation, as long as it is presented casually. Feelings of inferiority arise only when adults set artistic standards for children and try to teach them to draw.

When children first discover they can create marks, there tends to be an outbreak of scribbling on walls and furniture. Each time a new discovery is made, another burst of intense activity is likely and the drawing may show up in the wrong place.

Daryl's mother was surprised one day to see scribbling on Daryl's bedroom wall because she thought he had finished with that long ago. She was about to scold him when she noticed that the scribbles were a first attempt to write the letters of his name. Lisa, who had given up drawing on walls, discovered she could decorate herself. For several weeks afterwards, her arms, legs, and stomach were covered with artwork. These periods of overexuberant drawing usually pass quickly, as the child's desire to explore a new discovery becomes satiated.

## *Building*

As in drawing, the building efforts of the two-year-old show a distinct developmental progression. The toddler's energy seems to go primarily into knocking down towers that have been built by other people. However, toddlers are also developing important construction skills. They stack objects on top of one another, and they lay out toys in rows. In doing so, they are learning about two important building principles: balance and straight lines.

These ideas are explored further between the ages of two and three. Children discover how to make towers taller, more stable, and more pleasing to the eye. One method is to build a tower with objects that are of similar size and shape. When Trevor was given a set of blocks with different shapes, he intentionally stacked squares together, circles together, and triangles together, creating columns that were solid and attractive. Younger children sometimes utilize this principle, but more often their stacking is haphazard.

A second and more sophisticated way to design a tower is to place the larger shapes on the bottom and the smaller, less regular shapes on the top. This idea seems patently obvious to us as adults, but children do not learn it for some time. Toddlers try to balance the most unlikely combinations: a frisbee on top of a toy school bus which is on top of a peanut but-

ter jar. This kind of wild experimentation declines among two-year-olds as they learn to balance smaller objects on top of a larger base.

Whether the tower of a two-year-old looks like a smooth column, a delicate turret, or just a random collection, it usually is labeled. Jennifer, for example, considered her towers to be churches and castles. Beverly built a tall tower and described it as "the office where Daddy lives." Similar to the drawings of two-year-olds, constructions like these are hardly realistic, but the children have gained the insight that a real object can be symbolically represented by a set of blocks.

Just as towers get taller, lines get longer and they also begin to represent something else. Matthew lined up all his toy animals on the back of the sofa and called it a bridge. Constance made long lines of blocks and referred to them as trains. Peter put his Fisher Price people in a row and pretended it was

a parade. As these examples illustrate, two-year-olds are not limited to building lines with blocks. A line can be created with puzzle pieces, silverware, or beads on a string.

Sooner or later, the two-year-old who is interested in building lines makes a major discovery: the corner. Once corners become a possibility many different kinds of flat constructions can be built with line elements. A line can change direction, two lines can intersect, a line can keep turning until it forms an enclosure. With just a few suggestions or demonstrations, two-year-olds make a host of imaginary objects: fences, roads, beds, dance floors, and swimming pools.

The role of parents in building activities, as in drawing activities, is to strike a balance between demonstrating new ideas and allowing children to work on their own. Building a tower with a new element, such as a crossbar that becomes an imaginary diving board, may stimulate imitative efforts by a two-year-old. Building a simple network of roads may trigger more elaborate block play. The particular forms made by parents are inconsequential, for the goal is not to teach techniques of block building. The goal is to support two-year-old children as they explore building possibilities, and to share in their sense of discovery. The fun comes not just in the building, but in the conversation and imaginary play that follows.

Traditional construction toys such as Tinker Toys® and Lincoln Logs® are designed for children older than three. They require greater coordination and dexterity than the two-year-old possesses. However, the Tinker Toy idea—fitting a peg in a hole—does appeal to two-year-old children, and there are versions that are satisfactory.

Interlocking blocks, such as Duplos®, are available for building tower constructions. This type of toy is less flexible than a set of wooden blocks, but it may give the child a feeling of having built something more substantial. With any of these construction toys, two-year-olds seem to be primarily interested in learning how to connect the pieces, and less interested in experimenting with different forms.

# Imaginative Play

"Picnic's ready, everybody sit down. No, Big Bird, you sit up over here and don't fall down." As we watch Melinda, who is two and a half, arranging her "Sesame Street" characters around the picnic table, we get the feeling that we have just walked into the middle of an elaborate stage production. Melinda is a rather bossy director instructing the various characters as to how they should play their parts.

"Want a hamburger, Big Bird?" Melinda asks as she shoves a red crayon into Big Bird's beak. "Yes, I want a hamburger," Big Bird answers in a high squeaky voice. "So do I," answers Melinda, as she pours some imaginary ketchup onto a stack of poker chips.

Although adults may do their own kind of pretending, "pretend play" is the hallmark of childhood. Whether the youngster is surrounded by a roomful of Fisher Price® miniatures, or out in a backyard with nothing but a clothespin, the child's imagination creates its own special alchemy. The Fisher Price characters walk and talk and the old-fashioned clothespin is a soldier, an airplane, or a fishing rod.

In this chapter we describe imaginative play from three different viewpoints: The Development of Pretending, Different Styles of Pretending, and the Reasons for Pretending. Throughout the chapter we describe ways to encourage and enrich a child's pretending.

# THE DEVELOPMENT OF PRETENDING

During their second year, children make a significant transition from play that is primarily imitative to play that is primarily imaginative. As one-year-old toddlers jabber into a toy telephone or sweep the floor with an oversized broom, they are copying, as accurately as they can, a performance they have witnessed. But as children approach two years, subtle changes can be seen in their style of playing. Imaginary play episodes and themes begin to emerge.

As young as two years old, when she had just about mastered the two-word phrase, Kori's favorite play theme was a trip to Star Market. At first the trip consisted of slinging a purse across her shoulder, mounting her rocking horse, and chanting "Star Market." A few months later, a new element was added to the Star Market excursions. Kori recognized that Star Market was a place to buy things. Before mounting the rocking horse, she gathered up a paper bag and her favorite Raggedy Ann. "Go Star Market," she told Raggedy Ann. "We buy peanut butter, orange juice, cherries."

Within the next six months, Kori's language took a quantum leap and the trips to Star Market became much more complex. "Need a pencil and note pad, going to Star Market. You running out of peanut butter? You need margarine and paper towels?" Kori squiggled some lines on her notebook, gathered up Raggedy Ann, her mother's purse, a paper bag, and a set of keys. Struggling to carry everything in her arms, and seating herself on the top of a cardboard carton, she scooted along the floor. (The carton had replaced the rocking horse as her preferred mode of transportation.) "Vroom, vroom, vroom, going to Star Market. Mommy running out of peanut butter. Mommy running out of paper towels."

As we compare Kori's renditions of the Star Market excursion, we see changes taking place in the way Kori uses imitation. In the first version, the imitative component is predominant. Kori slings the pocketbook over her shoulder exactly like her mother. As the trips become more elaborate, Kori is no longer limited to simply mimicking her mother's actions. Now she can act out a routine that expresses her own notion of what going to Star Market means: Star Market is where you buy important things that are good to eat or good for wiping up spills.

A young child is apt to be confused by a trip to the supermarket and to see it as a sequence of unconnected experiences: a hurried exit from the house, a drive in the car, a place with

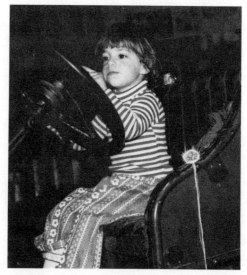

lots of noise and people, a cart with cans and boxes thrown in, a lady who rings a machine. As children return time and time again to the store, they begin to make sense out of these random impressions. Ultimately they realize that running out of food, driving to the store, putting food in the basket, giving the cashier money, and bringing the food home are all part of the same event. Each time children play out a new pretend sequence, they demonstrate this emerging ability to recreate a sequence and to make sense out of a complex occurrence.

The repertoire of play themes expands between the ages of two and three. Young two-year-olds play mainly at eating, sleeping, driving, and cleaning up while older two-year-olds include such activities in larger schemes. They go to the laundromat, the bank, the circus, or the zoo. They fish, camp out, go to church or to McDonald's. They may be gas station attendants, garbage collectors, taxi drivers, mail carriers, doctors, or sales clerks. The increase in the number of play themes is related to the child's expanding life experiences. As children go to more places, see more people, and do more things, they have an increasing variety of material to draw upon. The addition of new play themes also reflects a greater ability to organize and interpret new experiences.

Another development in imaginative play within the third year is an increased reliance on language. As children gain more understanding of language, they respond more readily to the suggestions of adults. At the same time, their greater ability to use language enables them to direct the action, furnish the dialogue, and supply the running commentary in a pretend production. The more adept the child is at using language, the more elaborate a production will become.

*Andrew: "Here comes the big truck. Watch out everybody, big truck coming."*
*Father: "Sorry, big truck. You have to slow down. You are coming to the toll gate. Here's your ticket, Mr. Truck Driver."*

*Andrew:* "Thank you, Mr. Man. Zoom . . . zoom, going up the mountain. Oops, flat tire."

*Father:* "Humm, that flat tire looks pretty serious. We'd better find the jack and jack up your truck."

*Andrew:* "Here's the jack. Fix the tire."

*Father:* "Let's hurry, looks as if you've got ice cream in your truck. We don't want it to melt."

*Andrew:* "Yeah—got lots of ice cream, and chocolate ice cream, and strawberry, and more ice cream."

*Father:* "You're making me hungry. How about giving me an ice cream sandwich while we repair this flat tire."

# DIFFERENT STYLES OF PRETENDING

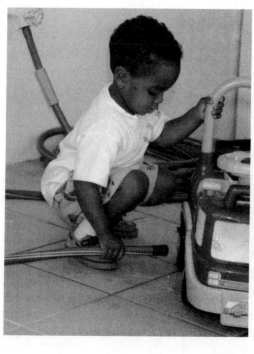

Over the third year you see there is a growing sophistication in the way children develop and play out a theme. Frequently we see two-year-olds who have developed a preferred style of pretending. In some of the families we visited, the dominant method of pretending was role play—adopting the role of someone else or playing out an imaginary experience. In other families, the major way of pretending was through the creation of an imaginary landscape and the animation of objects. We have labeled the first kind of play the actor style and the second the producer-director style.

## *The Actor Style*

The actor style play, where the child assumes a role, is by far the more popular with two-year-olds. When children begin role play they are likely to choose the role of mother or father. A first step in pretending to be a mother or father is to dress up in a parent's clothes. As young as eighteen months of age, youngsters love to sneak into their parents' closet or open up all their drawers. They try on hats, shoes, belts, and scarves. They adorn themselves with beads and bracelets or cover themselves with makeup. This dressing up is highly imitative. By their second birthday, however, a subtle change takes place. The children begin to imagine themselves in the parent role. "I am Daddy and you are a two-year-old," May announced, and you knew she had gone beyond imitation and was pretending to be the daddy.

Another very early way of assuming the parent role is to take care of a baby. The baby can be a stuffed animal, a doll, a puppet, or even a clothespin with a face on it. Like dress-up play, taking care of a baby starts off as imitation but evolves over time into a pretend activity. Almost every family we visited reported at least some caregiving play with a doll, puppet, or stuffed animal. Let's look at three representative scenes.

Heather, at two and a half, had a special corner in her bedroom which served as a dining room table for her baby doll, her Disney World characters, and herself. She had the table set for breakfast when we arrived.

"Daren, want juice? I give you juice. Want more juice? Want scrambled egg?" Heather poured some "juice" from the pitcher into the cup, and held it to Daren's mouth. "Mickey Mouse, you want juice, too, you want egg?" Heather jabbed the scrambled egg with a fork and brought it up to Mickey's mouth. Then she turned her attention to the baby dolls. "Here's bottle, baby doll. All gone, bottle all gone, baby doll." Heather took the bottle away, placed the doll on her shoulder, and tenderly burped it.

Linn Su, who is several months younger than Heather, started a caregiving episode by placing herself and Cookie Monster at a small table in the kitchen. First, she fed herself Cheerios with an occasional offering to Cookie Monster. Then she picked up the toy telephone and began to jabber. After several seconds, Linn Su put the telephone to Cookie Monster's ear and warned him in a strict voice, "Talk couple few minutes."

Angelina, who is about the same age as Linn Su, chose Howard Johnson's restaurant to begin her pretend play. While the family was waiting for dessert to arrive, Angelina's parents got into a conversation and were not paying attention to her. When they looked up, they discovered that Angelina had placed her Crying Tears doll face down on the table and had removed its clothes. "Clean up, clean up doo," she announced as she wiped Crying Tears's bottom with a paper napkin. After several minutes of vigorous wiping, Angelina unfolded the napkin and put it on Crying Tears. "Ah, ah, go sleep," but apparently Cry-

ing Tears was not quite ready for sleep. Angelina picked her up suddenly, crunched the napkin and went back to wiping her bottom. "Clean up doo, clean up," she continued in a still louder voice.

These examples of doll play illustrate some typical two-year-old ideas about the role of a caregiver. Caregivers cook food and feed others; that is, they control the food supply. They diaper babies, wash their faces, brush their hair, and are generally responsible for upholding standards of cleanliness. Finally, caregivers are masters of that wonderful invention, the telephone. Usually they talk on the telephone themselves, but occasionally this privilege is extended to their babies.

While two-year-old caregivers are likely to be affectionate, readily hugging and kissing their dolls, these "children-parents" can be harsh disciplinarians. Parents who have never used spanking as a disciplinary technique may be surprised to see their two-year-old energetically spanking a doll.

The children we have described so far played the role of caregiver by animating a doll. Another common way to try out this role is to switch roles with a parent and make the parent be the baby. "You the baby," Jeremy announced to his father, who had just come from work. "Sit down right here. I bring you drink of juice. You like juice?" Jeremy asked as he fed his father a cup full of air.

"No," his father muttered. "This juice is terrible; it's sour. I want a bunch of grapes."

"Here some grapes," Jeremy continued sweetly, after a quick trip to the hall, which apparently served as a kitchen.

"Oh, brother," his father complained. "These grapes have seeds in them. I think I would like to have some green seedless grapes."

Unperturbed, Jeremy went back to his storehouse in the hall. "Here some gweenless gwapes, Daddy."

Children who take the parent's role may not always react so calmly to their demanding babies. Erik decided one evening that he was the mother; and the rest of the family—mother, father, grandma, and grandpa—were all babies. Erik distributed "blankets" to each of his cast and announced, "Bedtime, everybody go to sleep."

"This is no blanket. This is a diaper. I want a blanket," complained Grandpa.

"Okay you take this blanket," Erik said, pulling away the blanket from his father and giving it to Grandpa.

"I want my blanket back," Erik's father howled in mock rage.

Then his mother joined in. "I want a bigger blanket. This one is too small."

Standing in the middle of the floor with his hands on his hips, Erik said firmly, "Try to be quiet and take your naps."

At two years old, both boys and girls like to play the role of mother. In the same way, girls enjoy playing roles associated with their fathers.

Suzanne: *"Need my lunch box. No butter please—gotta watch my clesteral."*
Mother: *"Your what? Oh, your cholesterol. Okay, I didn't put any butter on your sandwich." (Hands Suzanne the empty lunch box.)*
Suzanne: *"Bye, going to work, got to hurry." (Gets on Big Wheel® and drives from the kitchen to the living room.) "Vroom, vroom, vroom, got to go to work."*

Some two-year-olds also associate the father role with being the fixer. When we entered Frank's house, he was on the porch inserting the barrel of a toy pistol into a screw head on the window screen. As we watched him, he moved systematically from screen to screen inserting the gun into each screw head and giving it a quick twist. The entire operation was completed without a word. After each of the screws was tightened, Frank went to work on the caulking. Using his gun now as a caulking tool, he went about sealing the cracks in the screens. We asked Frank's mother how this intense interest in fixing got started. It seemed that her own father came to the house about once a month, tool kit in hand, and fixed everything that needed fixing. Frank would trail his grandfather for the entire day, cooperating as well as he could in each of the repair jobs. Apparently, Frank had decided that a father's role is to fix things.

Most of the two-year-olds in our study reflected conventional stereotypes in their actor-type play. Pretend mothers took care of the homefront while fathers disappeared to work. As more parents begin to share the roles of caregiver and provider, children's ideas about who disappears to work are changing. However, we expect that two-year-olds will continue to understand best the parent roles that are carried out within the home. Because two-year-olds are attracted to the home-based behavior of both their mothers and their fathers, it is a good time to provide a variety of props for parent play. Boys enjoy dolls, cooking utensils, and tea sets, just as girls enjoy cars, trucks, and tool kits.

Next to a mommy or daddy, the most popular role among two-year-olds seems to be a doctor. However, the doctor role is too complicated, and perhaps too frightening, for many two-year-olds to manage without help from older children and adults. We observed the following example:

Stacey, a four-year-old, picked up her two-year-old sister and stretched her out on the sofa. "You're the baby and I'm the doctor. I'm gonna make you all better so don't you move." Amy obediently waited while Stacey poked her with each of the instruments from her doctor kit and gave her several "just pretend" shots. At Stacey's suggestion, Amy even made pretend crying noises at the appropriate moments. Then, as soon as Doctor Stacey turned her attention elsewhere, Amy took over the doctor role. Her mother was selected as patient and each

instrument was used in succession just as she had seen her sister use them. At the end of the examination, Amy gave her mother medicine and an imaginary balloon. The whole procedure had progressed with little conversation, except that Amy provided the appropriate cue when it was time for her patient to cry.

Another role which many of our actor-type children played was being a waiter or waitress. Like doctor play, this pretend theme works best when an adult participates. Andy and his father provided a good demonstration. "I'd like a large green hot dog with corn ears," requested Daddy. "No man," Andy replied. "We don't got no hot dogs in this restaurant. You want a hamburger?" Father: "No hot dogs! What kind of restaurant is this? Do you have a cucumber and ice cream sandwich?" The game continued with much laughter.

Pretending to be a teacher sometimes appears in the imaginative play of a two-year-old. Again, the amount of elaboration depends on the child's familiarity with the role. Tania had an older sister who was in kindergarten, but she had no idea what really happened there. She did know that her sister took a lunch box to school. Setting Curious George on the kitchen table, she said, "Okay, I'm the teacher. Time for lunch. Open up your lunch box. Eat your lunch right this minute." Allison, a two-year-old who went to a small play group three times a week, had a different idea about what teachers do. Like Tania, she arranged her dolls at the table. "No, no, Baby Boo, no pushin'. How many times I got to tell you? No pushin'. Sit in the corner and don't you move."

In a sense, playing the role of a teacher, a waitress, or a store clerk represents an extension of the caregiver-mother role. The attributes of a caregiver are placed in a new and larger context. In the same way, being a garbage collector or an airplane pilot, which are occasional pretend themes with two-year-olds, is an extension of the fixer-driver-father role. It seems that two-year-olds fall back on the roles they understand best, the roles of mother and father, when they try to play out occupational roles.

Some actor-type children elaborate their imaginative play by taking a different approach. Instead of adapting the parent role to a new identity, they act out unusual events or experiences: a ride on a boat, a trip to the circus, a visit to the beach. With very few exceptions, these imaginary events never reach a culmination. As a matter of fact, most of the time they don't even get off the ground. The high point comes in the preparation.

"Going to the beach," Jennifer announced, as she sorted through the box of stuff in the corner of the room.

"Need the keys. Don't take the bus to beach. Take car. You want to go to the beach?" she asked her doll, wrapping it in a diaper and stuffing it into the carriage. "I want to go the beach," Dolly answered in Jennifer's high squeaky voice. "Wait for me," said Jennifer to the doll. "I've got to get packed up." Jennifer got busy filling a paper bag with an assortment of beach supplies: a toothbrush, a Green Stamp catalogue, an empty milk carton, a string of beads, a piggy bank, and a Mr. Rogers tape. "Got to dress me," she insisted as she struggled to get her arm in the sleeve of a smock. Satisfied with her own outfit, Jennifer found a hat for her doll and a hat for her

younger brother. "Want to be the daddy?" she asked her brother in a solicitous voice.

Jennifer's excursions to the beach never went beyond the packing up stage because the packing up stage became longer and longer. In contrast, some two-year-olds also extend imaginative play by introducing new events with chaotic rapidity. They skip from theme to theme, and from role to role, with little attention to continuity. Angeline provided a delightful example of this kind of versatile play.

When we first came into the house, Angeline was astride a blown up giraffe on the back porch. "Hurry up, horsey, hurry up, giraffe," she chanted. As soon as she saw us, Angeline picked up the giraffe and carried it into the living room. "Want a drink?" she asked, as she offered the giraffe a paper cup. Then she turned the giraffe on its side, felt it to see if it was dry, took its temperature with a spoon, and diapered it with a kitchen towel. When her mother turned on some music, she picked up the giraffe and danced with it around the room. As the music ended, Angeline turned her attention to the giraffe's tail. For some reason it reminded her of a barbeque grill. Angeline flipped an imaginary hamburger on the grill. "Hungry Mommy? Want lunch? You want ketchup?"

## Producer-Director Style

So far we have been looking at a style of imaginative play in which children are actors, portraying the role of a familiar character or playing out some interesting event. In either situation, they pretend by placing themselves directly in the imaginary scene. Another style of imaginative play that we see at this age is the producer-director style, which is somewhat more detached. The child stands back from the action and directs a pretend world. Sometimes, he animates a cast of miniature characters. At other times, the focus is on arranging an imaginary set. The favorite props for this activity are standard commercial toys: cars and trucks, farm animals, Fisher Price® people, miniature characters, and dollhouse furniture.

Kori had just returned from a trip to Drumlin Farm. Her mother had prearranged a farm scene on her bedroom floor

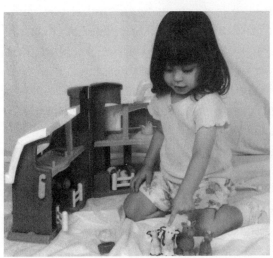

using a Fisher Price farm set. Kori examined the scene with intense interest. For several minutes she clutched her hands in a gesture of quiet excitement. "The horse is hungry," Kori's mother suggested. Kori crouched on the carpet. She put the farmer inside the toy wagon and pulled the wagon around in a circle. "You want milk?" asked the farmer who was driving the wagon. "Hm, thank you, glup, glup, glup," answered the horse. "Want more milk? Want some dinner? Pig want milk too?" Kori systematically pulled the wagon around the farm yard, providing the dialogue for the farmer and the animals in a highly squeaky voice.

Matthew, like Kori, frequently assumed the producer-director role in an imaginative play routine. He had been playing on the floor with Kermit the frog, a teddy bear, and a basketball hoop. When Kermit got stuck in the basketball hoop, his mother initiated the play theme by talking to the frog. "Oh, Kermit, you are hurt. Do you need to go to the doctor?" Matthew immediately answered, "Yes, he's hurt. Take him to the doctor." The doctor conveniently turned out to be a Teddy Bear who gave Kermit a purple medicine. Next Matthew began to make Kermit move around the room. He described the scene as the action took place. "Now Kermit's leg is all right. He's going to jump over the bed. He's going to jump in the tire, watch this!"

As we examine Kori's orchestration of the Drumlin Farm scene and Matthew's maneuvers with Kermit the Frog, it is obvious that a good deal of sophistication is needed to verbalize the play ideas of a producer-director. However, two-year-olds may set the stage with miniature characters without adding any dialogue. Marguerita, who is a relatively nonverbal two-year-old, had a package of miniature salt and pepper shakers and a set of Tootsie Toy® cars. While we were watching, she lined up the cars and put one or two of the shakers beside each car. We weren't sure she was pretending until her older brother asked if he could have a car. Marguerita put her arms protectively around the fleet and answered in a cross voice, "No, no! Fill up." "Oh," her brother interpreted, "she's filling her cars with gas."

The producer-director style does not necessarily require miniature people, animals, or elaborate props. It can begin with basic raw materials—blocks, crayons and paper, a ball of clay, or perhaps just words. Once children grasp the idea that they can set the rules in imaginative play and things can become whatever they want them to be, they are ready to devise their own story lines.

Our general impression is that the child who prefers the actor style is physically active, exploratory, energetic, and impulsive. The producer-director type is apt to be somewhat more reflective—planning out strategies and developing new ideas. It would be interesting to follow some of these children over time. Will the children who prefer the actor style grow up to be outgoing and social, while the producer-director types grow up to be more reflective and reserved?

# REASONS FOR PRETENDING

In attempting to describe the various kinds of imaginative play we find in two- to three-year-olds, we have selected examples that are particularly striking. These examples are not typical of all the families we visited. As a matter of fact, we found many children who were not interested in imaginative play at all. We asked ourselves whether imaginative play serves a developmental purpose, and whether it is an important factor in social, emotional, and/or cognitive development.

## *Making Sense Out of the World*

As we have already suggested, one reason children pretend is that it helps them make sense out of the world. As children play and replay familiar events, they understand them better. Let us consider once more the ever popular theme of food in the imaginative play of two-year-olds. The evolution of this theme illustrates the link between pretending and the development of new concepts.

At just over a year we see the beginning of pretend eating. One toddler lifts an empty cup to his lips or gives his daddy a pretend bit of dinner; a second toddler makes believe that she is picking a grape off the fruit design on her mommy's blouse. By the middle of the second year, many children have expanded this theme to include the preparation of food. They make cookies out of sand, mix a birthday cake in an empty bowl, or crack pretend eggs on the side of a pan. A further extension, usually in the early twos, involves serving the food. This is the well-known tea party stage, in which the child plays hostess to people, dolls, or stuffed animals.

From this point on, the food theme can be expanded in several directions. Many children at two and a half or three get interested in pretending to buy food at the grocery store. Some children recognize that before you go to buy food, you have to make a list of what you need. Other children recognize that you have to get money before you go shopping and so they stop off at the bank on the way to the market. Still other children go on a picnic, plan a barbecue, or eat out in a restaurant.

Looking at the various expansions and extensions of the food theme, we recognize how many different concepts can be associated with it. Two-year-old children are constantly accumulating additional experience with the process of buying, preparing, and eating food. By observing the kind of pretending that a two-year-old organizes around food, or any other recurring theme, parents can infer what new ideas are of greatest interest to their child. They are then in a better position to help their child explore and clarify these ideas.

Imaginative play helps two-year-olds make sense out of the world on a more abstract level as well. As children become familiar with a specific imaginary theme, they begin to recognize, at least in that limited context, the difference between reality and fantasy. One indication of this process is the appearance of joking behavior in imaginative play. In the beginning, pretend ideas tend to be carried out in a serious manner. The child who is just learning to set up a tea party or go on an imaginary shopping trip is likely to be quite solemn. But when the pretense becomes well-established, the child becomes more playful. A pretend routine can even become a ritualized joke. Whenever Kyle's father sat down to read the newspaper, for example, Kyle began a teasing game. Looking at his father and laughing, he would pretend to take huge bites out of his father's tie.

Another sign that children are distinguishing between reality and fantasy is the use of the word "pretend." Parents who introduce a word like "pretend" as they play with their two-year-olds usually find that their children pick up the term quickly. Once the two-year-old is familiar with the term, it becomes easier to discuss situations in which the difference between reality and fantasy is unclear. Imaginary thinking has both power and limitations. It can create a powerful imaginary experience, but not directly change the real world. As children play out a variety of themes, and as parents talk to them about their pretending, children begin to appreciate this paradox.

## Compensating for Feelings of Inadequacy

Another explanation for imaginative play is that it provides children with emotional support. At times, children play out scary events until their fears are under control. The kinds of fears that plague the two-year-old often appear to be irrational. Parents told us of two-year-olds who were afraid of butterflies, beards, egg shells, fire sirens, Band-Aids, or Santa Claus. Zachary would not go to sleep at night because he was afraid that a cow would jump on the roof and crash into his bedroom.

As we think about the two-year-old's growth, we recognize that these fears are the product of the child's ability to create mental pictures, to imagine things that are not present. The same developmental advance that gives children the power to play out imaginary themes also makes them fearful. They can imagine all sorts of inanimate things coming to life—stuffed animals, trees, the moon, or clothes hanging in the dark.

Gregory was terribly afraid of lions. Several times during the night he would run into his parents' bedroom, screaming that a lion was after him. At the same time, he insisted that his mother and father read a story about Johnny Lion at bedtime. He even took a little stuffed tiger to bed with him. At first glance, it might seem better for Gregory's parents to discourage reading the book and sleeping with the tiger. In actuality, this pretending seemed to help Gregory cope with his fear. With experience controlling imaginary lions and tigers, he would be less likely to be plagued by nightmares.

There usually is a close link between feelings of fear and feelings of excitement. Experiences that are exciting can be frightening as well. Being pulled in a wagon is great fun up to a certain speed; beyond that, it is terrifying. Being pushed in a swing is tremendously exciting up to a certain height; beyond

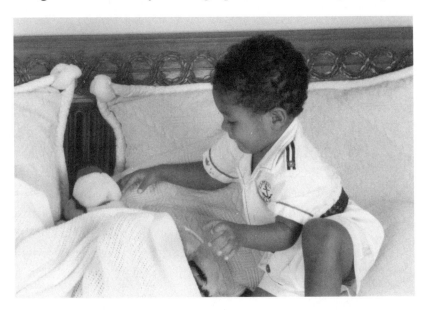

that, it, too, is terrifying. With their new powers of imagination, two-year-old children can anticipate a fearful situation before it exists. A child who likes quiet dogs but is afraid that frisky dogs might jump on him may begin to whimper at the mere sight of a dog across the street. A child who is interested in fire trucks but afraid of loud noises may become alarmed by the faintest sound of a distant siren. In cases like these, the children's imaginations have run away with them and blocked out the excitement of the real situation.

Although parents are concerned about the fears of their two-year-olds, this fearfulness is a sign that the children are ready for more pretending. Imaginative play may tip the balance back from a frightening experience to an exciting one. With the child who cringes at the sight of the neighbor's dog, parents can introduce a stuffed dog who keeps jumping on everyone. The child who cries at the sound of a distant siren can be given a fire truck and parents can introduce a siren game. "Rrrrrh," the parent wails as the child sits in the bathtub. "Here comes the fire engine to put out a fire." The fire truck roars up the side of the bathtub and along the edge,

straight toward the watching child. "Ooops," the parent mutters as the fire truck careens into the bath water. "The fireman had an accident, his siren's broken . . . blub, blub, blub, blub."

Imagination also can deflect feelings of loneliness and insecurity. Almost every two-year-old we visited had a favorite doll, stuffed animal, or security blanket. These loved items kept the child company in new and strange situations. At an early age, children are not very selective about the kind of thing they choose for a companion. Several of our young two-year-olds were attached to such odd items as screwdrivers, shampoo bottles, or whisk brooms. These objects seemed to be almost animate. The children would insist on taking them along on rides, bringing them to the table, and going to sleep with them. Occasionally parents even heard children talking to these strange companions. "Bye-bye, have to go to store now," Jason said to a new pair of shoes in his closet.

The animation of unlikely objects seems to decline between the ages of two and three, but the animation of dolls and stuffed animals gets even stronger. At Halloween, Erik adopted a large skeleton decoration as his companion. "Look at shoe," he exclaimed with excitement, pointing to the bones in the skeleton's foot. "Mr. Skeleton nice man, he wants eat, too," Erik said. After a large chair had been provided and Mr. Skeleton draped over it, Erik decided that his new companion wanted to eat soap. Later in the day it looked as if the skeleton had been forgotten on the floor, but Erik informed his parents, "Be quiet. Skeleton taking a nap."

## Developing Social Skills

A third benefit of pretend play is the acquisition of social skills. As they pretend together, children learn to engage others in their fantasies. They cooperate, negotiate, take turns, compromise, and build on each others ideas. Two- to three-year-olds who are good at pretending are likely to be chosen as playmates by their peers and even accepted by older children. In the preschool years, the children who are good pretenders tend to be the most popular.

Although there are important benefits in pretend play, two-year-old pretending is not always appreciated by adults. In a small minority of the homes we visited, imaginative play was frowned upon. It was thought of as a mechanism for avoiding the truth, and children who indulged in imaginative play were scolded for telling lies. A second group of parents, also a minority, tolerated imaginative play but felt that it took away time from more important things like learning numbers and letters. A third group, and by far the majority, felt that imaginative play was important and sought out ways to encourage it. We were especially interested in these families and identified two characteristics that they had in common:

- There were adults or older children who had a special interest and talent for playing imaginatively with the two-year-olds.
- A variety of materials were available for imaginative play and parents allowed children to gather their own props and create special places for pretending.

## FOSTERING PRETEND PLAY

For two-year-olds, the greatest inducement for pretending is to play with an adult or older child who enjoys it. As we visited with different families, it was easy to identify the parents who were especially interested in their child's imaginative play. These parents described with obvious pleasure the pretend games they enjoyed with their children.

Brandon's family is a clear example of a family that took advantage of their youngster's readiness to play imaginatively. As we walked into the family room, the first thing that caught our eye was a giant wooden structure which took up a good third of the room. This structure was a playhouse built to order by Brandon's father. It served as a store, a castle, a jail, a puppet theater, and as just a good hiding place. Obviously, the family had a great time with it.

Watching parents play with their children, we could see that parents, like children, have preferred styles of imaginative play. Some parents prefer to be actors. They participate in a very direct way in their child's pretend themes. Others are definitely the producer-director types, gathering props, suggesting dialogue, drawing pictures, telling stories, or making up rhymes and songs. Finally, we found the appreciative-audience parents—those who love to watch their children's pretend activities but do not participate very often.

Parents who were skilled in actor-type play knew how to be opportunistic. At just the right moment, they asked a question or made a comment that served to initiate an imaginative play sequence.

*Shawn was sitting on top of his red car making a "vroom vroom" noise. His father, who had been talking to us, turned to Shawn.*

*"Hello, Mr. Shawn. I see you are out in your red Corvette. Are you running a bit low on gas?"*

*"Filler up, please," Shawn responded. (Obviously this was not the first time father and son had enacted this scene.)*

*Shawn's father pretended to fill the car with gas. "Do you want me to check the tires? Your right rear looks a bit low on air."*

*Shawn watched as his father pretended to check the tires.*

*Shawn: "How much I owe you?"*

*Shawn's father: "Ten dollars even."*

Shawn pretended to take the money out of his pocket and put it in his father's hand. He drove off with a humming sound but was back two minutes later for a repeat performance.

Annie's mother, like Shawn's father, very much enjoyed actor-type play. Her particular forte was pantomime. While we were there, she and Annie acted out a pretend game using gestures. Annie was playing in her outgrown cradle which her mother had placed on the floor. As Annie climbed into it, she said, "Boat." Her mother took advantage of the moment. "Let's go on a boat trip," she suggested, climbing in the cradle beside Annie. "We'll see if we can catch a fish. Throw out your rod." At this point Annie's mother went through an elaborate pantomime. She threw out her line, caught a fish, tossed it into the boat, and wiped off the splashes from her face and arms. Annie was very attentive. Obviously she could not follow the whole routine, but she enjoyed watching her mother's performance.

In many of the homes we visited, an older sister or brother joined in actor-type play. In most cases this worked very well. The two-year-old was delighted to be included in the act and was willing to accept any part. Naturally the younger child was assigned a passive role while the older child provided the lead

ership, but at the first opportunity the two-year-old tried to take a more active part. We were amazed at how adept two-year-olds could be in following a play routine. Frank, for example, took over the role of teacher when his sister left the room. "This is a A," he told Pooh Bear, as he showed him a W. "Say it now, say 'A'. Say 'A' nice and loud so I can hear you."

Many parents who enjoyed being producer-directors helped set up fancy playscapes: a Disney World theme, a gasoline station, a zoo. Others selected less grandiose stage settings and concentrated their efforts on making puppets or animals talk. Timothy's mother was a most effective director type. She was sensitive to Timothy's inquisitiveness and his interest in replaying a new experience. Timothy had gone on a picnic with his grandfather at a state park. When Timothy came home, he went to the play corner of the family room where all his toys were kept. There, on a low table, he found his little "Sesame Street" people. Big Bird, Ernie and Bert were arranged around a "picnic table," which was a red and white checked paper napkin. Beside the picnic table was a small basket full of bits of junk. Without encouragement, Timothy began to direct the show.

"Want a hamburger, Ernie?" Timothy asked, as he served Ernie a delicious cork coaster. "No, Ernie, no more ketchup. You want ice tea? We don't got ice tea. Want hot dog? Mommy need cook it." Timothy was now pulling his mother's jeans.

"Need what?" his mother asked, puzzled by the request.

"Need cook it," Timothy repeated insistently. "Need cook it, hot dog."

"Oh, you need to cook your hot dog. You need a barbecue."

"Yes, need cook it."

Timothy was delighted that his mother had understood him. He was perfectly satisfied with the empty juice can she gave him to use as a barbecue.

As we watched Timothy and his mother, it was obvious that this kind of pretending was quite typical. Although Timothy's mother did not get into the act, she knew just which props would get Timothy started. She also accepted Timothy's rules for pretending. Invisible hot dogs were fine to serve to Bert and Ernie as long as they had been cooked on an appropriate grill.

## *The Props*

Whether or not parents are direct participants in an imaginative episode, they play a key role in helping two-year-olds find appropriate props. It was interesting for us to see how creative parents became when they got involved in gathering props. For example, we saw three different ways of providing a picnic lunch. One parent filled a picnic basket with pictures of food from a magazine. A second parent filled a shoe box with empty jello, raisin, and cereal boxes. Still another parent used bread dough to make a variety of play foods.

Of course, prop gathering, especially when the job is taken over by a two-year-old, has drawbacks. Parents kept telling us about keys, extension cords, credit cards, and pot lids appearing in the oddest places. Typically these treasures were to be found in a special, private place for pretending. This place, selected by the children, was likely to be too small for adults to enter but just right for small children. Examples that parents mentioned were: under the kitchen sink, behind the sofa, the knee hole of a desk, under a card table with a sheet over it, inside the fireplace, on top of a bunk bed, and under a toddler table.

In order to facilitate prop gathering, we have developed two lists. The first includes props that are most conducive to actor-type play. These props correspond with the different ways children may choose to act out a role.

## *Things to Put On*

- Hats of all kinds
- Makeup and felt tip markers
- Belts, ties, beads, bracelets, watches

- Grownup shoes, boots, slippers
- Old clothes, smocks, shirts, raincoats

## Places to Go

- Large boxes
- Blankets or sheets that can be thrown over a table to make a tent
- Porches

## Things to Carry

- Pocketbooks and billfolds
- Lunch boxes
- Shopping bags
- Suitcases and briefcases

## Things to Use

- Toy telephone
- Keys
- Small notebook and pencil
- Bits of string and ribbons
- Dolls, stuffed animals, and puppets
- Thermos
- Real or toy pots, pans, dishes, utensils
- Old typewriter or cash register
- Assorted small boxes or containers
- Poker chips, small blocks
- Tongue depressors
- Old photographs

The second list includes props that especially encourage producer-director type play.

- Playscapes
- Playhouses
- Farms
- Doll houses
- Restaurants
- Toy villages
- Miniature railroads

## Miniature Toys

- Small cars, trucks, and planes
- Miniature characters

## Raw Materials

- Boxes and baskets
- Squares of fabric, linoleum, tile, or rugs
- Blocks
- A heavy tag board or pegboard square to use as a roof or floor
- Crayons, watercolors, and inexpensive paper
- Chalkboard and chalk
- Flannel board or Colorform sets

We have looked in a systematic way at the ingredients of pretend play—the interested parent, the appropriate props, the special play space. But even with these ingredients, imaginative play cannot flower without a foundation of real-world experiences. The more meaningful experiences children have, the greater their potential for play. Children cannot understand what a prop stands for unless they are familiar with what the props represent.

A toy is representative of something in the real world, but if children have not experienced the real world, they have difficulty with the analogy. Most of the important experiences for two-year-olds are the everyday routine events: getting dressed, eating, cleaning up, going to the grocery store, taking a bath. Some salient experiences, however, are out of the ordinary events: a trip to the zoo, an airplane ride, a Thanksgiving dinner. Still other salient experiences come from television and books.

The emergence of imaginative play in two-year-olds is an exciting phenomenon, but it needs to be put in proper perspective. Two-year-olds are just beginning to take advantage of the

potential of pretending. Their imaginative play is not yet very sophisticated. They pack up for a trip to the beach and never leave the house. They feed the dolls a birthday cake and then blow out the candles. Most of their pretend themes are simple and cannot be elaborated without help from older people. In fact, quite a few two-year-olds do minimal pretending. In some cases, they are busy with other developmental tasks: mastering motor skills, manipulating objects, and interacting with different people. In other cases, they do not yet have the verbal skills to extend an imaginary theme. Whatever the reason for their lack of pretending, it is not irreversible. With time and parental support, all children can reap the benefits of imaginative play, extending the boundaries of space and time, experiencing new powers, and exploring their own creativity.

# *Index*

~~~~~~~~~~~~~~~~~~~~~~~~~~~~~~~~~~~~~~~

## Q

## R

## S

# About the Author

~~~~~~~~~~~~~~~~~~~~~~~~~~~~~~~~~~~~~~~~~~~~~~~

MARILYN SEGAL, PH.D., a developmental psychologist specializing in early childhood, is professor of human development and director of the Family Center at Nova Southeastern University in Fort Lauderdale, Florida. The mother of five children, she has written thirteen previous books, including *Making Friends* and *Just Pretending*. She is also the creator of the nine-part television series "To Reach a Child."

# Parenting and Childcare Books from Newmarket Press

**Baby Massage**
*Parent-Child Bonding Through Touching*
Amelia D. Auckett; Introduction by Dr. Tiffany Field

A fully-illustrated, practical, time-tested approach to the ancient art of baby massage. Topics include bonding and body contact; baby massage as an alternative to drugs, healing the effects of birth trauma; and massage as an expression of love. Includes 34 photographs and drawings, a bibliography, and an index. (128 pages; 5 ½" x 8 ¼"; paperback)

**How Do We Tell the Children?**
*A Step-by-Step Guide for Helping Children Two to Teen Cope When Someone Dies—Updated Edition*
Dan Schaefer and Christine Lyons; Foreword by David Peretz, M.D.

This invaluable book provides straightforward language to help parents explain death to children from age two through teens. It includes insights from psychologists, educators, and clergy. Special features include a 16-page crisis-intervention guide to deal with situations such as accidents, AIDS, terminal illness, and suicide. "Parents need this clear, extremely readable guide . . . highly recommended." *(Library Journal)* (192 pages; 5 ½" x 8 ¼"; hardcover & paperback)

**Inner Beauty, Inner Light**
*Yoga for Pregnant Women*
Frederick Leboyer, M.D.

In matchless prose and stunning photographs, Frederick Leboyer discusses the importance and beauty of yoga for pregnant women. He shows how they can use yoga to move toward healthy and joyous childbearing, and how the health benefits will far outlast the birthing process for both mother and child. "Frederick Leboyer is that rare modern combination of scientist, mystic and poet." *(Newsweek)* (276 pages; 8" x 10"; paperback)

**In Time and With Love**
*Caring for the Special Needs Baby*
Marily Segal, Ph.D.

Sensitive, practical advice on play and care for the preterm and handicapped child. Includes information about daily care, interacting with siblings, coping with doctors, discipline, social skills, and tough decision making. Also included is a special section on activities to promote emotional development and encourage motor and language skills. "This book accomplishes its goal of presenting an honest picture of what it's like to live with a difficult baby." *(Journal of the Association for Persons with Severe Handicaps)* (208 pages; 7 ¼" x 9"; hardcover & paperback)

**Loving Hands**
*The Traditional Art of Baby Massage*
Frederick Leboyer, M.D.

In *Loving Hands,* Frederick Leboyer uses his deep insight into childcare, as well as knowledge gleaned from his travels in India, to show us how, in the weeks and months following birth, we can use the flowing rhythms of the art of baby massage to communicate our love and strength to our babies. "Leboyer puts the baby into psychological focus. He conveys his message with superb photography and poetic language." *(Psychology Today)* (144 pages; 8" x 10"; paperback)

**Mothering the New Mother**
*Your Postpartum Resource Companion*
Sally Placksin

This all-in-one resource guide covers everything from homecare options, help for breastfeeding problems, and workplace negotiation strategies, to adjusting to full-time motherhood, postpartum depression, and hiring a doula. Each chapter is filled with practical suggestions, hands-on solutions;,and an invaluable listing of the newsletters, books, hotlines, videocassettes, support groups, services, and caregivers available to the new mother. Includes checklists, planning sheets, an index, and resource guides. (352 pages; 7 ¼" x 9"; paperback)

## My Body, My Self for Boys
*The What's Happening to My Body? Workbook for Boys*
Lynda Madaras and Area Madaras

Packed with drawings, cartoons, games, checklists, quizzes, and innovative exercises, this book encourages boys to address head on their concerns with their body, body image, height, weight, growth, hair, voice changes, reproductive organs, sexuality, emotional problems of puberty, diet, and health. Winner of the *American Library Association* "Best Books of the Year" Award. (128 pages; 7 ¼" x 9"; paperback)

## My Body, My Self for Girls
*The What's Happening to My Body? Workbook for Girls*
Lynda Madaras and Area Madaras

The companion book to *The What's Happening to My Body? Book for Girls*, this workbook/diary encourages girls ages 9 to 15 to explore their feelings about their changing bodies. Everything affected by the onset of puberty is covered, from body image, pimples, and cramps, to first periods, first bras, and first impressions. Includes quizzes, checklists, exercises, and illustrations. (128 pages; 7 ¼" x 9"; paperback)

## My Feelings, My Self
*Lynda Madaras' Growing-Up Guide for Girls*
Lynda Madaras with Area Madaras

For preteens and teens, a workbook/journal to help girls explore their changing relationships with parents and friends; complete with quizzes, exercises, letters, and space to record personal experiences. Includes drawings and a bibliography. (160 pages; 7 ¼" x 9"; paperback)

## Raising Your Jewish/Christian Child
*How Interfaith Parents Can Give Children the Best of Both Their Heritages*
Lee F. Gruzen, Forewords by Rabbi Lavey Derby and the Reverend Canon Joel A. Gibson

This pioneering guide details how people have found their own paths in Jewish/Christian marriages, and how they have given their children a solid foundation to seek their own identity. Includes a bibliography and an index. (288 pages; 5 ⁵⁄₁₆" x 8"; paperback)

## The Ready-to-Read, Ready-to-Count Handbook
*How to Best Prepare Your Child for School—A Parent's Guide*
Teresa Savage

A step-by-step guide that shows how to teach preschoolers basic phonics and numbers. Over 60 phonetic learning exercises, 35 games, homemade flashcards, 24 assignments, and a series of cartoons encourage a tension-free, fun-filled environment while your child develops skills in motor ability, logic, listening, and comprehension. Includes a bibliography, an index, and reference lists. (272 pages; 5 ⁵⁄₁₆" x 8"; paperback)

## Saying No Is Not Enough
*Helping Your Kids Make Wise Decisions About Alcohol, Tobacco, and Other Drugs—A Guide for Parents of Children Ages 3 Through 19*
Robert Schwebel, Ph.D.; Introduction by Benjamin Spock, M.D.

This acclaimed book is the most recommended guide for parents to help them meet the growing problem of "kids and pot" as well as other drug prevention issues. Since its initial publication in 1989, health education and parenting experts have recommended the book for its wisdom and practical advice. "Wise and wondrously specific: a solid parenting manual." *(Kirkus Reviews)* Includes a bibliography and an index. (304 pages; 6" x 9"; paperback)

## The Totally Awesome Business Book for Kids (and Their Parents)
Adriane G. Berg and Arthur Berg Bochner

Everything kids need to know about business with special attention to jobs that help the environment. Introduces vital business skills such as research, telephoning, negotiating, complaining when appropriate, making contracts, filing, and record keeping. Includes illustrations, a bibliography, and a glossary. (160 pages; 5 ⁵⁄₁₆" x 8"; paperback)

## The Totally Awesome Money Book for Kids (and Their Parents)
Adriane G. Berg and Arthur Berg Bochner

For young readers from ten to seventeen, this fun, fact-filled guide uses quizzes, games, riddles, stories, and drawings to teach the basics of saving, investing, borrowing, working, taxes, and more. Includes illustrations, a bibliography, and a glossary. An *American Library Association* "Best Book of the Year" finalist. (160 pages; 5 ⁵⁄₁₆" x 8"; hardcover & paperback)

## The What's Happening to My Body? Book for Boys
*A Growing Up Guide for Parents and Sons—New Edition*
Lynda Madaras with Dane Saavedra

Written with candor, humor, and clarity, here is much-needed but hard-to-find information on the special problems boys face during puberty. It includes chapters on the body's changing size and shape, hair, perspiration, pimples, and voice changes; the reproductive organs; sexuality; and more. "Down-to-earth, conversational treatment of a topic that remains taboo in many families." *(The Washington Post)* Includes drawings, charts, diagrams, a bibliography, and an index. (288 pages; 5 ½" x 8 ¼"; hardcover & paperback)

## The What's Happening to My Body? Book for Girls
*A Growing Up Guide for Parents and Daughters—New Edition*
Lynda Madaras with Area Madaras

Selected as a "Best Book for Young Adults" by the *American Library Association*, this bestselling book provides explains what takes place in a girl's body as she grows up. Includes chapters on the body's changing size and shape, the reproductive organs, menstruation,; and much more. Includes drawings, charts, diagrams, a bibliography, and an index. (304 pages; 5 ½" x 8 ¼"; hardcover & paperback)

## Your Child at Play: Birth to One Year
*Discovering the Senses and Learning About the World*
Marilyn Segal, Ph.D.

Focuses on the subtle developmental changes that take place in each of the first twelve months of life and features over 400 activities that parent and child can enjoy together during day-to-day routines. "Insightful, warm, and practical... expert knowledge that's a must for every parent." (T. Berry Brazelton, M.D.) Includes more than 250 photographs and a bibliography. (352 pages; 7 ¼" x 9"; hardcover & paperback)

## Your Child at Play: One to Two Years
*Exploring, Daily Living, Learning, and Making Friends*
Marilyn Segal, Ph.D.

Hundreds of suggestions for creative play and for coping with everyday life with a toddler, including situations such as going out in public, toilet training, and sibling rivalry. "An excellent guide to the hows, whys, and what-to-dos of play." *(Publishers Weekly)* Includes more than 300 photographs, a bibliography, and an index. (288 pages; 7 ¼" x 9"; hardcover & paperback)

## Your Child at Play: Two to Three Years
*Growing Up, Language, and the Imagination*
Marilyn Segal, Ph.D.

Provides vivid descriptions of how two-year-olds see themselves, learn language, play imaginatively, get along with others, make friends, and explore what's around them. It give specific advice on routine problems and concerns common to this age group. Includes more than 175 photographs, a bibliography, and an index. (272 pages; 7 ¼" x 9"; hardcover & paperback)

## Your Child at Play: Three to Five Years
*Conversation, Creativity, and Learning Letters, Words, and Numbers*
Marilyn Segal, Ph.D.

Hundreds of practical ideas for exploring the world of the preschooler, with sections devoted to conversation, creative play, learning letters and numbers, and making friends. Includes more than 100 photographs, a bibliography, and an index. (288 pages; 7 ¼" x 9"; hardcover & paperback)

# Parenting/Childcare Books from Newmarket Press

Ask for these titles at your local bookstore or use this coupon and enclose a check or money order payable to: **Newmarket Press**, 18 E. 48th St., NY, NY 10017.

*Baby Massage*
_____ $11.95 pb (1-55704-022-2)
*How to Help Your Child Overcome Your Divorce*
_____ $14.95 pb (1-55704-329-9)
*How Do We Tell the Children?*
_____ $18.95 hc (1-55704-189-X)
_____ $11.95 pb (1-55704-181-4)
*Inner Beauty, Inner Light: Yoga for Pregnant Women*
_____ $18.95 pb (1-55704-315-9)
*In Time and With Love*
_____ $21.95 hc (0-937858-95-1)
_____ $12.95 pb (0-937858-96-X)
*Loving Hands: Traditional Baby Massage*
_____ $15.95 pb (1-55704-314-0)
*Mothering the New Mother, Rev. Ed.*
_____ $16.95 pb (1-55704-317-5)
*My Body, My Self for Boys*
_____ $11.95 pb (1-55704-230-6)
*My Body, My Self for Girls*
_____ $11.95 pb (1-55704-150-4)
*My Feelings, My Self*
_____ $11.95 pb (1-55704-157-1)
*Raising Your Jewish/Christian Child*
_____ $12.95 pb (1-55704-059-1)
*The Ready-to-Read, Ready-to-Count Handbook*
_____ $11.95 pb (1-55704-093-1)

*Saying No Is Not Enough, Rev. Ed.*
_____ $14.95 pb (1-55704-318-3)
*The Totally Awesome Business Book for Kids (and Their Parents)*
_____ $10.95 pb (1-55704-226-8)
*The Totally Awesome Money Book for Kids (and Their Parents)*
_____ $18.95 hc (1-55704-183-0)
_____ $10.95 pb (1-55704-176-8)
*The What's Happening to My Body? Book for Boys*
_____ $18.95 hc (1-55704-002-8)
_____ $11.95 pb (0-937858-99-4)
*The What's Happening to My Body? Book for Girls*
_____ $18.95 hc (1-55704-001-X)
_____ $11.95 pb (0-937858-98-6)
*Your Child at Play: Birth to One Year, Rev.*
_____ $24.95 hc (1-55704-334-5)
_____ $15.95 pb (1-55704-330-2)
*Your Child at Play: One to Two Years, Rev.*
_____ $24.95 hc (1-55704-335-3)
_____ $15.95 pb (1-55704-331-0)
*Your Child at Play: Two to Three Years, Rev.*
_____ $24.95 hc (1-55704-336-15)
_____ $15.95 pb (1-55704-332-9)
*Your Child at Play: Three to Five Years, Rev.*
_____ $24.95 hc (1-55704-337-X)
_____ $15.95 pb (1-55704-333-7)

For postage and handling, please add $3.00 for the first book, plus $1.00 for each additional book. Prices and availability are subject to change.

I enclose a check or money order payable to **Newmarket Press** in the amount of _____

Name _____

Address _____

City/State/Zip _____

**For discounts on orders of five or more copies or to get a catalog,**
contact Newmarket Press, Special Sales Department, 18 East 48th Street, NY, NY 10017;
Tel.: 212-832-3575 or 800-669-3903; Fax: 212-832-3629.